The Leisure Wasters

The

Leisure

Wasters

by
Connie O'Connor

South Brunswick
New York: A. S. Barnes and Co., Inc.
London: Thomas Yoseloff Ltd

A. S. Barnes and Co., Inc.
South Brunswick, N.J.

Thomas Yoseloff Ltd
18 Charing Cross Road
London W.C.2, England

6413
Printed in the United States of America

41,696

Introduction

I am not one who is much interested in writing exposés. I would much prefer to write either inspirational ravings on all the opportunities that life offers, or scholarly volumes on the theory of leisure.

I am by nature a cockeyed optimist who would be happy pounding out words about all the joys waiting out there in Leisure Land. But I can't blind my eyes to truth. All is not well. There are strange things lurking in leisure. As I have studied and examined the sociology and psychology of leisure I have seen these things and they have "thrilled me— filled me with fantastic terrors never felt before." They are things that may turn leisure into a Leisure Wasteland, a land we may all visit at some time or another.

This Leisure Wasteland has existed in the past, exists now and will exist in the future. We have all seen it. We have seen self-pity and bitterness swallow up hours of leisure. We have seen exercise being obtained through the tempter tantrum; novelty and change being sought through love affairs; and escape from tension being found in drink. The time: Leisure.

I have lived in a working girls' residence and seen the vast supplies of leisure being wasted there. I saw girls who were living the most barren of leisure lives. These girls were young, attractive, and healthy. They were looking forward to having something exciting to write home about, but none of them seemed to be finding such excitement. Of the 60 girls in one residence that I lived in, not more than four had any notion of an interesting way to spend Saturday morning, afternoon or evening. Sunday really died. They all appeared to be waiting for a Prince Charming to take them away from all that monotony, but failed to recognize the fact that spending all one's leisure time in a girls' residence is not the way to find a man.

What about the young, unmarried, male side of the Leisure Wasteland? What did they do? Among the servicemen at the local U.S.O., I noted more young people who had positively no ideas of how to spend their off-duty time, unless they were drinking, loafing around the barracks, or picking up girls. There didn't seem to be too much enthusiasm displayed about those possibilities, either.

Take the young family, just buying their house, television, car, rugs, last three babies, and all major kitchen appliances. I have lived among them and seen them moping their way through leisure. I have seen young wives shriek to their husbands that they had to get away, and then get away by driving the unpaid car around for hours until the tension was gone.

I have been in the homes of people living the last years of life; living in homes so utterly silent it was like living in an atmosphere magnetized with loneliness and monotony.

I have also been exposed to the problem of alcoholism, the great executioner of leisure time. I have witnessed excessive student study, where students read until they had a headache, then drank coffee and read magazines because they couldn't fall asleep at night.

I have seen young isolated mothers looking out of their split-level homes and marveling at the fact that there was a life going on outside, a life from which they felt totally separated. I have travelled and seen people spend thousands of dollars *not* to enjoy themselves.

But let's begin our trip. On to the Leisure Wasteland. We have many miles to go, and the woods are lonely and dismal.

Contents

The Leisure Wasters

1.

The Leisure Wasteland

The Leisure Wasteland
Population: 190 million people at one time or
another. (A tourist spot. Some stay minutes,
others months, others stay for years.)

This book is written for leisure wasters. It is *not* written
for married college students paying their own way through
school by working eight hours a day, studying eight hours
a day and waiting for the baby to cry for the other eight
hours. This book is *not* written for the laborer who digs
up sewer pipes all day and spends the evening at another
job in order to support his seven children.

Nor is this book written for dentists who go cave explor-
ing on weekends, attend a square dance club and fencing
class during the week, and entertain friends on Wednesday
evenings. This book is not written for the engineer who
reads history as a hobby, sings in the church choir, weekends with a hiking club, and is president of the local stamp
collecting group.

This book *is* written for leisure wasters. It is written for
all who have ever had a tweak of conscience that told them
that they were wasting their leisure time.

Tweakers—Read on.

There seems to be a confusion as to what the word lei-sure, means. I recall a woman who wrote me a nasty note after I had written to her, asking her to supply me with some information of her service organization. I told her that it was for a "Leisure Directory." She replied, "This organization is definitely *not* leisure. All the members are devoted and hard working women who would be outraged to hear you call us a leisure group. Of all the nerve!"

According to the Oxford English Dictionary, leisure is:

Freedom or opportunity to do something specific or implied. In a narrower sense: Opportunity afforded by freedom from occupation.

A current philosopher of leisure states:

Leisure, however we shall later characterize it, deals with hours and ways of behavior in which we are freest to be our-selves. Thus, what we do, whether on the noblest of levels and aspirations or the lowest of tastes, is a clue or indication of what we are, who we are, where we want to go. . . . In our leisure we stand exposed.[1]

And what an exposure! Leisure time is a stage on which many a rogue can perform. The characters of a bad lei-sure: nervous tension, drinking, lovers, boredom, busy-work, frozen feelings or the inability to care deeply about anything, extended work, loafing, marital unhappiness. All these problems can perform during leisure time, and there is no bothersome interruption from work.

Let's take a look at a few wasteland scenes.

The garbage man is given a picture of the wasteland as he totes the whiskey bottles away. The motel owner sees a double exposure of the problems of leisure. Lonely hearts club directors are anything but disheartened. The divorce courts are filled with results that might not have occurred if we were not gifted with leisure time, and tranquilizers go down as nervous tension goes up.

Pleasure neurotics are working overtime to avoid play. Vacant eyes are returning from $2,000 European tours through 12 countries in ten days. Weekend travelers are finding that highways can be wreck-reational for nerves. People who never before had time, are discovering that they now have the leisure time to think about why they should commit suicide, and in Los Angeles you can spend your leisure calling Suicides Anonymous and be told why you shouldn't do away with yourself. Some leisure is spent skating over frozen feelings, or trying to defrost them through high stimulus methods.

Motion Mania is the fast way through boredom, while frenzied living and busywork both offer similar opportunities for the devout leisure waster. You can literally shake time away through nervousness. Wasting one's talents through non-use offers satisfaction to those with destructive urges. Tossing and turning all night gives the daytime sofa loungers an excuse to sleep all day. A lack of awareness as to what's going on in the big world is the painless way to waste leisure, while a constant searching for "the action" can take up all kinds of leisure time. Friend "hopping" is also time consuming.

Let's get down to figures. What is leisure in terms of actual hours?[2]

		Hours
There are 365 days in a year		8760
Deduct 8 hours a day for sleep	2920	
Deduct 5 days' work a week at 8 hours a day for 49 weeks (allowing 2 weeks' vacation and seven other holidays)	1960	
Deduct 2 hours a working day for travel	490	
Deduct 3 hours a day for meals	1095	
Deduct 1 hour a day for dressing and undressing	365	
	6830	8760
		6830
Hours left to do with as we please		1930

The above adds up to 22 percent of the year, or 80 days or 24 hours each. Where do all these lovely hours go? They are largely wasted in many ways. Given more leisure, there probably would be more waste.

However, we all want more leisure. The word has become glorified, but the reality of the word may be a miserable experience.

We make sure that we never receive all this leisure time, however. Very cleverly and perhaps unconsciously, we arrange things so that we cannot possibly have any leisure hours to enjoy. We kill leisure before it is born.

Strong words? Let's itemize.

Item one: Given more time free from vocation we spend more time getting to the location. It seems to follow that once our working hours are reduced, we lengthen the distance from our home to our work. Thus, we waste the time that we save by spending an extra half hour traveling to work.

Item two: We have been blessed enough to live in an economy that gives each person more money. As soon as we get it, we involve ourselves in debts that imprison us as much as poverty could ever do. Does a bill laden person ever seem to relax in leisure?

Item three: On one hand we are told that we are going to be gifted with more leisure. Be happy and enjoy it because it is the result of our countries high production and wealth. On the other hand, leaders of the "anti-frill" movement are urging that we eliminate from our educational system all the courses that may make our leisure worth living at some future date. So we go to school and receive training that will enable us to earn a living for seven hours a day, but don't learn how to live a productive life for the remaining hours. "Training for a living, but not for "living" may actually be the war cry of the zealous few who seem so interested in perpetuating the work ethic (which slowly may be going out of existence).

Item four: Our beautiful schools, parks and recreation centers with their music chambers, theatres, and gymnasiums—not fully utilized. Why aren't these areas in *full-time* operation? Why aren't adults and children learning their leisure possibilities from A to Z? Where are all the people? Chalk up a point for waste. Wasted opportunity occupies every empty school.

Item five: The family. It has been suggested that with additional leisure, the family will have its greatest hour. There will be the laughter and the excitement of family participation. In actuality, leisure seems to be offering the family more time to engage in open conflict. Tensions long held at bay by "apartness" have too much time to break through even the most muscular repressions. Husbands and wives can bicker more. Children have more hours a day to get on parents' nerves.

A Gallup Poll taken in 1957 indicated that women were opposed to the four day week by a three to one margin.[3] Another study of 50 married couples indicated that husbands attach more value to leisure time than do wives.[4] What could be the reasons for the hesitancy to accept leisure on behalf of wives? One reason could be that although women would probably like more leisure, they know that more leisure for their husbands does not mean more leisure for them. Household tasks and child care will still take time and the housewife may find herself at work while her husband "lives" his leisure. Maybe women are afraid husbands will get in the way more, or drink more, or run around. Whatever they fear, women do not seem to be as much in favor of the new leisure as men appear to be. However, men are not in favor of more leisure if it means more "honey-do" days (Honey do this, honey do that).

Item six: Taking care of one's possessions. This is another area where people demonstrate the inclination to destroy their own leisure. As soon as labor saving devices are invented, or work hours are cut, out runs harried Harry to buy a large house with a large lot and thereby states to all the world that he will never be available because of all the chores that need to be done. It would cost him less in time, effort, and anxiety to hire a highschool boy to help out, but Large Lot Larry wants no help. "I'd rather do it myself," he states in tones of true martydom. Large Lot may then be heard to complain about all his chores. Suggest to him that he sell the house and buy one with less acreage, he will look horrified and blurt out, "But what would I do with all that free time?"

Another type of leisure laborer buys expensive equipment that's more expensive to maintain than the original cost. This equipment then procedes to dictate to him how he will spend his leisure. This demanding item may be a boat that needs to be scraped or a pool that must be cleaned. It may be some kind of mechanical hobby that needs excessive care.

I recently was informed of one man, who has a collection of beer mugs that extends from the house to the garage. He spends hours every week just dusting and cleaning those mugs, while constantly complaining about the effect of the Los Angeles smog on his collection.

If maintenance is performed happily, that's fine. If it's a grind and source of complaint, that's something else.

It would appear that there is a great deal of hypocrisy in our general attitude toward leisure. Our view of it is usually through rose colored glasses, while in reality it can be a truly miserable condition.

When we talk about the *individual* and leisure, we see many varieties of leisure expenditure. We find that the individual personality makes the difference between good and bad leisure use. Some people are unhappy anywhere. Others are radiantly happy under even the most deprived of environments.

Proof for the above statements can be found in a city such as San Francisco. San Francisco is an ideal place for the productive and educational use of leisure or for the pursuit of a wide variety of interests. Yet, loneliness and misery exists in the boarding houses and apartments of San Francisco that could equal any of the rungs of Hell portrayed by Dante. Jean Paul Sartre says that "Hell is other people," but my observations in San Francisco would seem to indicate that Hell is a lack of other people. The loneliness truly was a means of suffocation.

Most of the 200 or more people that I lived among in boarding houses would have stated that life in the big city was a very dull affair indeed. Most of these were young and attractive people. Many spent leisure barrenly for a short period of time only, and then learned how to spend it in a more satisfactory manner. Others never learned.

If one were to take a trip through the homes of these young and unattached people, one could hear the cry of boredom. It is most ugly and pathetic when it appears in the young, however. It seems amazing that boredom and loneliness should be the way of life of these very young, working people who have the freedom, money and attractiveness that could be put to better use. The main problem seems to be that these young people, newly away from home, do not seem to know where to start, how to start or why it is so necessary to learn to live with their free time. They have no friends to begin with; are shy and reluctant in pushing themselves forward in some strange group; and though they want to participate in life, they just do not seem to have the motivation to do so. So they just sit or sleep. It seems amazing, but a close observation of the situation would bear out the fact. There is a leisure wasteland all around us.

People seem much more inclined to work for a living than they are to work on *living*. What are some of the signs by which the leisure waster may be known? How can we be aware of the fact that ourselves or others are failing in leisure? Here are some symptoms:

Boredom (accompanied by shallow breathing and frequency of loooonnnnng sighs).
Headaches and general irritability.
Sluggishness.
Tendencies to cry easily, periods of nostalgia.
Guilt feelings over not using time better.
Excessive worrying over little things, over nothing in particular.
Sleeplessness.
Feeling that life is passing us by.
Feelings of isolation, insecurity and non-belongingness.
Constant gloom and despair.
Disgust with our lazyness, feelings that we are *unable* to act.
Anger, cause unknown.

When any of the above take up much of a person's time, it is not difficult to see how there would be an enormous sidetracking of energy. Such emotional exercises drain this energy, leaving the individual exhausted and tense.

One sociologist has written of the "Great Emptiness" of leisure and states that for many people, leisure time holds nothing in store. Several kinds of people experience this emptiness, coming with leisure and ending when work returns. One kind is the go-getter. The go-getter experiences it mildly, however, since he really doesn't ever stop working. He just keeps working and accumulating more and more money.

Another kind of person experiencing the emptiness of leisure is the average man. This is the person who has had little training for leisure and who usually has no strong interests or devotions. Most people fall in this category.

The religious cult followers are lucky in that their great emptiness has been filled through a kind of hypnosis. They, perhaps, experience it the least painfully.

The biggest emptiness and the most painful, exists for those persons who live for some worthwhile end. They are the idealists. They could be great artists, writers, thinkers. They aim high and when they miss the mark they become disillusioned and fall back on the great emptiness created by their idealistic reach. Their life is probably the most pathetic because they are left without their dreams.[5]

Other writers have stated that, given more leisure, all classes of society would become more and more alike in a mass culture, or would participate in unwholesome activities. One writer has come out most vehemently against the mass leisure that will be available through the communications media. He feels that it would appeal to lower tastes, would be sensationalistic and would thereby receive wide circulation. "Good" television would appeal to so few that it would be quite costly. The cost factor would thus eliminate "good" presentations from the scene. Result, mass culture on a very low level. "And they all look just the same."[6]

Another philosopher of leisure states that the working man will turn his new leisure into "body recuperation" even though he only works six hours a day. He will rationalize that he "needs" rest, remembering the past when man rested on his time off and overlooking the fact that resting days were necessary when one worked 12 hours a day, 6 days a week. This *resting* will not be what is most needed by the 6 hour a day worker, however.[7]

It would be a dizzying experience to conjecture about how many Liza Doolittles we have in our leisure wasteland today. How many of our recreationally deprived, with the help of a Professor Higgins, could raise themselves to enjoy a leisure that would contain only a small percentage of the bottle, extra sex-ular activities or extended voyages to dreamland. How many want to get out of the "lowbrow leisure class"?

Russell Lynes has broken leisure down (in cartoon form) into Highbrow, Lowbrow and Middlebrow "classes." Strictly *Lowbrow* are Western movies, beer, pulp comic books, and shooting craps. At the top end of the scale is the *Highbrow* with his Bach, Art League membership, avant-garde literature, and ballet.[8] And in between is a whole range of activities just right for getting people out of the leisure wasteland and onto the road to Life after work. Incidentally, the most common question of the Leisure Age may be, "*Is* there a life after work?" There is, but it takes reaching for.

Maybe we need the spirit of an Unsinkable Molly Brown to help lift us out of the leisure slum. Maybe we've got to believe that there is something better. Molly wants to be up where the action is, and whatever Molly wanted—Molly got!

Or maybe we need a dream, a dream such as the one MaMa in "Gypsy" had. A dream to be better than the commonplace, a dream to live. MaMa seems to be shrieking of her desire to leave the leisure wasteland when she sings about all the things *she* wants to do and see.

The leisure wasteland is inhabited by many types of people on any given day. *Everyone spends some of their leisure there* (at some time or another). Let's begin our tour through the Wasteland. Let's see some of the places that you have been—at one time or another.

2.

Work on the Rocks

Pleasure is a threat to many Americans. They
go to any lengths to avoid it. They abhor free
time because it is necessary to fill it with fun.
To paraphrase Shakespeare: Out of this flower,
leisure, they pluck this nettle, duty.—NORMAN
LOBSENZ[1]

Some people simply refuse to accept leisure. They have
the usual reasons for liking to work. They are:

1. Salary.
2. Feeling of identification with the larger, more productive
   society.
3. Companionship.
4. Feeling of identification with the specific work unit to which
   one is attached.
5. Social approval because one is engaged in something useful
   to society.
6. Gives one a frame or orientation, a home base.
7. Regularity, organization of activity. Gives one a sense of
   security.

Certain jobs probably lack some of the ingredients of job
satisfaction stated above. Automation has helped to destroy

feelings of satisfaction in the ultimate product on behalf of the worker, who often feels his contribution is very small indeed. Other types of employment offer very little security. Some employment has little in the way of companionship, while other occupations seem to involve too much socialization. Whatever are the factors involved in the joy of work, most people like to work. Or is it that they just hate not to work?

But let's return to people who refuse to accept leisure. According to them, work is the only way to fly. They are *miserable* in their leisure hours and can hardly wait to get back to the grind again. What are their reasons for refusing leisure? Here are a few possibilities:

1. Don't need relaxation because of strong work satisfaction.
2. Fear the excesses that may lurk in leisure, such as drink or sex.
3. Puritan influence will not let them relax. They have to work because they feel guilty about play.
4. Unhappy family or living situation that causes leisure to be a time for conflict games.
5. Not aware of any interesting leisure activities.
6. Extensive bills allow him very little leisure money.
7. No friends to engage in leisure interests with.
8. Bad past experiences which do not lead to pleasant anticipation of leisure.
9. Fear of boredom, lack of variety of activity, isolation.
10. No skills. Can't dance, swim, play any sport.
11. Other-directed leisure. Person just goes along to please someone else.

Betty J., age 36, unmarried. Works as receptionist in doctor's office. Very attached to the doctor, she experiences a sense of service that she feels is somewhat akin to the way she would feel if she were a wife. She considers herself an aid and a very necessary one. Her leisure seems empty away from her job and she spends it in a kind of limbo, anxiously waiting until Monday when she can return to the patients she enjoys meeting and the young doctor to whom she feels so strongly attached.

William B., age 20, unmarried. Works as a lather's assistant. Has no interests, little vitality. Feels free time is a drag and tries to get as much overtime as possible. Has recently learned to drink as a leisure pastime and is at times very frightened over the rowdy behavior he displays when drunk. "I can't decide which is worse though, being drunk or being bored."

George H., 55, married. Teacher in private school. George is not close to anyone in his family. He has four children, all in their early teens. Though his children are the same age as children he teaches, George feels that there is more companionship and respect at the school than at home. He has no friends (adult) and his wife directs his leisure with a firm hand. He tries to please her to avoid conflict.

All of the above are Leisure Wasters in the worst sense of the term. They *live* for the employed hours of five days a week. In leisure they go into deep freeze. They are not the same people as they are at work.

Norman Lobsenz, author of *Is Anyone Happy?* calls these people "pleasure neurotics." The "pleasure neurotic" sees leisure as a threat, and tries to fill as many hours as possible in "worthy" employment. Equipped for work, the "pleasure neurotic" is lost when not at work.[2]

One writer has stated that this type of pleasure escapee is like a plane that must keep on flying because it has no landing gear. The landing gear in this case would be the skills, interests, or attitudes necessary in order to be able to enjoy leisure time. To stop work might mean that they would be expected to relax, to enjoy themselves, to have fun. *Fun* is a word that gives the "pleasure neurotic" severe anxiety. He feels quite guilty about fun. Part of this guilt goes back to their early training in "keeping at the grindstone."

Sociologists have called this tendency of the middle class child rearing process, the *deferred gratification pattern*. The child is told to "study and work hard" and "don't let up because you've got to keep your eyes on your goal if you're going to get ahead." "Defer pleasures!" "Don't fool around!" "Be serious!" "Now is not the time for fun!"

Fun time just never does seem to come when one has had just a little bit too much of the deferred gratification pattern. A pleasure neurosis may develop and life becomes just one long succession of work—goal—job. No rest for the weary.

Bill W., age 30, married. Bill is a possible "pleasure neurotic." Any leisure time period finds Bill in a highly anxious state. He begins to itch, feels extremely irritable and finds fault with the way his wife keeps house to such an extent that she has stated that they must either go to a marriage counselor, or she will leave. Bill's interests are all engaged in very seriously. He is an expert on the violin, history and French cookery. He feels his wife is much below him in the area of leisure interests, as she has no special talents or abilities. When the family must spend time together, such as on holidays or anniversaries, and Bill cannot engage in his avocations, he falls into this state mentioned above. He finds it impossible to enjoy the activities of family life, and does not particularly like social events. He likes to have a goal to work for and attain, then set up another one and attain that. When he is forced to cease, even for a short while, in his efforts to work toward this goal, he becomes very obviously distressed. "My husband is a very hard man to live with," declares his wife. "He always has to be engaged in activities where he can grow. He never wants to share in an interest and rarely shows affection or gives of himself in any way other than sex. That is performed in a more businesslike than loving fashion."

One writer has stated that leisure implies an attitude of non-activity, of inward calm. It means not being busy, but letting things happen. Can you imagine the struggle of the "pleasure neurotic" to *let* things happen instead of *causing* things to happen? It is behavior decidely opposite to that elicited by his work experience. It is going against the grain of everything they were ever taught. It says "let up" instead of "keep going." Such advice is very hard for the DGP (Deferred Gratification Pattern) victim to follow.

Psychiatrist Alexander Reid Martin says:

One way a pleasure neurotic has of dealing with this situation is to take a rest, go on a holiday, play games, have recreation—but always proceed to be rather miserable and unhappy and see to it that there is no enjoyment. The principle here is that you don't have to pay in guilt for what you don't enjoy.[2]

This problem is not a new one. Psychoanalyst Sandor Ferenczi discovered a phenomenon that he called "Sunday Neurosis" some 40 years ago.

Ferenczi observed that many of the patients coming to him had headaches and stomach disorders that occurred on Sunday. This kept them from enjoying their day of leisure. When work started, the aches and pains cleared up. Ferenczi felt that the physical problems were a way out of facing a period of time with nothing to do. "After all, if I have a headache I really *can't* enjoy myself, can I?" A good excuse has come to the rescue.[3]

Are the very powerful tycoons in business, or the leaders in various professional fields leading the truly ideal life, a life worthy of emulation by those lower down on the occupational ladder? Sloan Wilson in *The Man in the Grey Flannel Suit* does not appear to come to this conclusion when he has his main character, Tom Rath, choose wife and family over the chance for a top broadcasting position. This he chooses after seeing the "top man," alone and without wife and daughter, using work as a way of getting the love and admiration that was absent in his personal life.

The top gun in *Executive Suite* also was alone and lonely, although on top of the prestige pile. He was painted as an all work and no play type. He bought friends, and only needed them in a "yes man" capacity. His life was just a series of goals, that he met, or else!

There may be room at the top, but is that the only place where true satisfaction is? There can be no leisure to worry about when one is completely immeshed in work problems and goals.

Leisure is something you "just don't think about" to many professionals who are deeply involved in their work. They don't have time to think about it or to plan for it. When it does come they find it painful enough to make sure that they don't get into it again.

I recall an interview I had with a successful radio station manager. He was full of zest, enthusiasm and good spirits as long as we discussed the radio business. When the subject of leisure came up he stated tersely that he had none and didn't want any. His expression was one of fear mixed with disgust and it was quite obvious that this was an idea he kept tightly repressed. When I remained too long on questions concerning retirement, this very friendly and sociable fellow felt I was going too far and almost asked me to leave.

My radio friend must feel like he is the little Dutch boy with his finger in the dyke. But sooner or later the flood is going to prove too strong and overwhelm him in spite of his efforts to forestall it. Leisure will come. Retirement is at the end of every work line, unless death should intervene. Perhaps there are many who would want it so.

One survey recently conducted on "moonlighting" (second job), pointed out that there were some who hailed "moonlighters" as heirs to the spirit of the nation's founders and insisted that hard work never hurt anybody. The pursuit of happiness to them is the pursuit of work.[4]

The pursuit of work is fine when some effort is channeled away from the occupational world and into the leisure world. Why can't the energy be switched from long hot hours over the briefcase to long tedious hours spent learning how to "appreciate" music, art, or literature. Why can't the work lover give up time analyzing reports of sales progress and turn such time over to perfecting a tennis serve, or learning some difficult guitar chords? There can be a great deal of work to play, and there need never be retirement.

David Riesman states that when among some committee-men he found himself feeling uncomfortable when discussing leisure. He says, "As with sex, they wanted to make a joke of it. And there is no doubt that most of us feel vulnerable in a milieu that increasingly asks us whether we are good players as well as good workers."[5]

William Faulkner comments:

One of the saddest things is that the only thing a man can do for eight hours a day is work. You can't eat eight hours a day, nor drink eight hours a day, nor make love eight hours a day—all you can do for eight hours a day is work. Which is why man makes himself and everybody else so miserable and unhappy.[6]

Bertrand Russell speaks next:

Broadly speaking it is held that getting money is good and spending money is bad. . . . The individual in our society works for profit; but the social purpose of his work lies in the consumption of what he produces. . . . We think too much of production, and too little of consumption.[7]

And so it will be, when as a society we take our work on the rocks. A nation on the overtime wagon is a nation headed for leisure skid row. We must get off the wagon. We must learn to get the same values from play that we get from work. Anyone for tennis?

3.

Members of the Bored

In its simplest terms, the primary problem of
leisure is how to avoid boredom.—RUSSELL LYNES[1]

Some people are not good workers, nor are they good
players. They fall into a kind of laissez-faire category that
could be named "The Time Trinklers." With them, time
seems to just trinkle away, and nothing much ever seems to
get accomplished.

The behavior of these bored people is characterized by
an aimless, apathetic sort of activity. They resemble something that the cat dragged in. They haul their zestless forms
around from one hour to the next, investing minimal interest in anything. "Life is a drag" seems to be their bore call,
just as "work" is the war call of the pleasure neurotic.

Their energy has literally been bored to death.

Is this a result of our automated age? Is this boredom
a result of our tensions, compartmentalized living or lack
of enough oxygen in the air? We may give many excuses for
it and attribute it to the "bad age we're living in," but we

are only blinding ourselves to the past, for boredom has existed in every age and time.

Russell Lynes, in a magazine article, mentions the fact that the leisure class of the 1850's had a number of scions of wealthy families who were so bored that life seemed not worth living. They felt that the only way out was to throw themselves into rivers, ending boredom (as well as their lives).[1]

You can trace boredom through history, and wherever you find the leisured wealthy, you will find a few members of the bored. In our rapidly approaching "leisure age," where not just a *few* will belong to the "leisure class," there is likely to be the same long sigh of boredom that existed back in the days when *most* people worked while *some* people played. "I'm bored!," seems to be the "in" thing to say in some groups today.

The fact that boredom may be growing in popularity is reflected by many of the recent magazine articles concerning this subject. Consider these titles:

Boredom: The Hidden Enemy
How to Cure a Case of Boredom
Trailing Clouds of Boredom Do They Come
Psyche of the Future (Boredom)
Boredom, Brainstorms and Bombs
Pathology of Boredom
Loneliness and Boredom
Is Boredom Bad for You
Why Be Bored
Lonely Wife
Heavy, Heavy, What Hangs Over
Simple Art of Never Being Bored

These articles have all appeared in big magazines. They all repeat the same problem over and over—Boredom. If all you knew was what you read "in the papers," you would know that boredom is all around us. Perhaps it's one of the fringe detriments of leisure. . . . and of a leisure where people find "nothing to do." Ho hum.

But just what *is* boredom? Why should it be? What is the cause? Consider this experiment at McGill University. It should bring some proof for the need of variety in daily life.

To test for the effects of monotony in people exposed to an isolated and unchanging environment, several students were selected for an experiment. They were to lay in bed 24 hours a day with time out for meals and toilet necessities. The students were given tests before and after confinement and in almost all cases the subject's performance was impaired by their isolation in the monotonous environment.

What changes in personality took place? First of all, as time went on the students became markedly *irritable.* When they came out for meals they were overly *talkative,* appeared *dazed* and *confused.* They experienced a *restlessness* that they described as being "unpleasant." *Hallucinations* occurred in which some saw dogs (and one saw many different kinds of eyeglasses). The individual's *thinking became impaired* and he showed *childish emotional responses.*

That's boredom. They were literally bored to tears, or temper outbursts, or strange behavior.

Hallucinations, incidentally, are quite compatible with monotony and isolation. Studies at Harvard have indicated that they are common among long distance truck drivers. People in isolated outposts have been known to see spiders as large as dogs and strange prehistoric animals. Charles Lindbergh has described some interesting hallucinations that took place on his long trans-Atlantic flight.

You may ask, "Who cares about people in isolated outposts? I've got people all around me, all the time. That's the trouble." You may have people all around, and still experience the effects of monotony. Translate the McGill experiment into a weekend that you might spend with a few silent, bored companions and you may see a similarity of results. There may not be hallucinations, but there will certainly be a good amount of irritability, fogginess and restlessness . . . with a few childish displays of emotion thrown in just to add a little excitement to a dull period. Perhaps it is lack of variety that is the cause of the tensions and outbursts that flare up between members of a family who have been too long in household pent. As one member of the McGill experiment declared: "Variety is not the spice of life, it is the very stuff of it!."[2]

What else, in addition to a lack of variety, could cause boredom? Aldous Huxley states that it is a result of the failures and disillusionments of politics, war, and nature's destruction by industry. He says:

A more subtle cause of the prevalence of boredom was the disproportionate growth of the great towns. Habituated to the feverish existence of these few centres of activity, men found that life outside them was intolerably insipid. And at the same time they became so much exhausted by the restlessness of city life that they pined for the monotonous boredom of the provinces, for exotic islands, even for other worlds—any haven of rest.[3]

Let's bring in a medical opinion now. Dr. Henry Ray, specialist in medical diagnosis and author of several books says:

Time after time I've examined a body that shouldn't be dead. I ask myself, "What killed this person?" and I find no answer in the organs. The heart, liver, kidneys—all are good for another 25 or 30 years, so far as I can tell. But the person died. He just lost the will to live. Nothing to look forward to.[4]

It appears that it is literally possible to be bored to death. But boredom can do worse than cause death. It can ruin life. In the 1930's Otto Fenichel gave this psychiatric opinion when he said that boredom was "the damming up of instinctual tensions and the repression of human aim and objects."[5] In short, it stops one's life energy.

Perhaps boredom is the result of man's failure to satisfy some of his basic personality needs. Eric Fromm has been very interested in "needs" and has devoted a great deal of study to them. He feels that they arise from the conditions of man's existence. Without satisfaction of them, man fails to find great satisfaction in life. Here they are, according to Fromm:[6]

1. Need for Relatedness—To be close to nature, especially one's own.
2. Need for Transcendence—To rise above one's animal nature, become creative.
3. Need for Rootedness—To feel that one belongs.
4. Need for Identity—To be recognized as a unique individual.
5. Need for a frame of reference—A stable way of perceiving the world.

Many recreations do not come close to satisfying any of these basic needs of man. It is in our recreations that we need to make an effort to choose activities that will "round" us out. This is *compensation time*. If we do not have time during our work day to get close to ourselves, but must be constantly garbed in "persona" as Jung would say, we need to let down our masks in leisure time to experience who we really are. If our work doesn't offer us a chance to think and be creative we must compensate for this in leisure. If we lack feelings of real "Belongingness" in our vocational lives, we need to seek areas where this feeling can be found. We may also feel a sense of identity when we feel we belong, but if we don't we can use our leisure to find areas where we can be recognized as unique individuals. In leisure we may attempt to find some stable way of perceiving the world apart from work. We may choose activities and friends that could remain stable and help us through rough periods of work or home life.

In our leisure we may meet ourselves. We may learn how to participate in life with our "whole selves." Perhaps boredom is partly caused by a lack of exercise of all our capacities and needs.

Can we exercise all our capacities and needs in front of the television set, at a cocktail party, on a luxury travel tour? There generally is a great deal of "waste of self" about all these recreations. A small part of the total person is invested. There is a mild climate of boredom throughout the activity. Have you noticed?

Let's take the luxury tour as an example. This tour would appear to satisfy certain needs such as the need for status or the need for change. It separates one from one's natural surroundings, however, and it tends to indulge the quest in his animal nature rather than transcend it. There's a feeling of non-belonging rather than rootedness. The frame of reference is one that is looking out on an ever-changing world, and if the individual is insecure, he can feel very disoriented against this perpetually moving backdrop.

I recently took one of these tours to Hawaii, and was amazed at all the apparent boredom I saw. Many of the travelers appeared in a trance-like state. Some were bewildered by all the new sights. Others slept throughout the limousine tour, undoubtedly lulled to dreamland through the noise and motion of the motor. There was much evidence of irritability, especially between husbands and wives. Some were constantly complaining, and the complaints ranging from "I get so darn tired of getting in and out of tour busses," to "There's just really not much to do, all we do is sit around and stare at things."

Why is the tourist so bored? Is it because he is situated

ten floors up, in an air conditioned, thickly carpeted, sound-proof hotel? Is it because he is too stuffed with delicious food and doped into insensitivity through exciting drinks? Is it because there are so many people around and yet he does not get to relate to any of them except on a usually superficial level? Is he tired of being a flight number?

Naturally, not all tourists are bored. The sad thing is that there are so many who are. They take a trip to their leisure wasteland and it costs them several thousand dollars. They do have something to talk about when they get home, however. This gives travel more status in the leisure waste-land than sleeping would have.

One magazine writer, referring to Americans' traveling,[7] stated that we rush here and there from monument to monument as if we were on a point system and had to make so many points per day. Wonderful sensations flood the body if we catch Old Faithful just before she goes off. Then we won't have to wait another hour. Hurry, hurry, schedule, snap. . . . "Oh be sure to get in the picture, Honey, we want the folks back home to know we were here."

Many people in their boredom like to spend money fast. In Australia, "Antiboredom Clinics" have been sug-gested by a church leader. It would be designed to help curb the recent gambling craze that is spreading through-out Australia. An Anglican Bishop there feels that bore-dom is the cause of gambling.[8] People want to "do" some-thing, move fast, go. Throw your money on the table! Watch the wheel! Excitement! Speed! It's one way to get rid of the oppressive sense of boredom.

"Antiboredom Clinics" may be one way of getting away from the boredom monster. August Heckscher, in his book *The Public Happiness* suggests that one solution may be in our mood of approach. Instead of *pursuing* leisure, we might *taste* it. The general attitude would be one of acceptance to new experience. We would then accept the world as it is and thus respond to leisure personally and spontaneously. Says Heckscher:

We have entertainment and distraction, but we have lost the sense of play, which is at the heart of a leisure society, for life is a kind of game.

Are we too determined, and not relaxed enough, to be able to enjoy anything? Do we relax our overly motivated systems when duty hours cease? Can we be passive to fun? If not, you may apply for membership in the bored:

REQUIREMENTS FOR THE BORED

Each member has:

1. A disbelief in leisure planning.
2. An unawareness of activity possibilities.
3. Excuse making talent.
4. A feeling that variety is for nervous people.
5. An idea that you are the last person that you want to know.

Here are a few statements of some bored members:

Bill M., age 45, married. Successful engineer. "Sure, I've got a big house, nice kids and wife and all kinds of sports equipment. But I'd rather work than be laid up with this broken foot. For a month I've been looking out of the window, wondering what life is all about. Life means to work. I really know that now that I can't work."

Willa C., age 25, single. Secretary. "Vacation periods for me are extremely boring. In trying to analyse the situation I have come to a few conclusions. In the first place, I never plan for my vacations. Then when they turn up I take a day to rest. I get up feeling terrible. I've had too much rest! I don't feel like doing anything then and so just sit around and get into such a rut that I do believe that I'm incapable of getting out of it."

Jill H., age 35, married. Housewife. "With the kids in school and my husband away on sales trips I should qualify for presidency of the bored. I'm missing out on something, but I'll be darned if I know what it is. There must be more to life than kids, housework, television and an occasionally-around-the-house husband."

James I., age 59, married. Retired surgeon. "This retirement business is really ridiculous. I would not have done so, but my hands are not as steady as they used to be, so I felt that I should retire and enjoy my money a little. But there's nothing really I want to do. I can't even fix myself something to eat because the cook will get upset. My wife would never let him go—or the gardener either for that matter. I read a great deal, but that gets tiresome. Reading is a wonderful thing and I don't want to ruin my love for it by excessive use. I don't care too much for any sports activity. The days are too, too long for me. I know I'm terribly bored, but I don't know what to do about it.

Boredom rarely attacks those who have an awareness of the diversity of activity available for them during leisure. The above members of the bored lack ideas. The more they stay with boredom, the more difficult it will be to escape. There are many, many things to do with leisure. As Auntie Mame said: "Life is a banquet and most poor fools are starving to death."

If leisure is like a smorgasbord table, then bread and butter people are going to miss out on a great deal. The newspaper, yellow pages of the phone book, adult education class schedules, city organization and club pamphlets are ways to find out what is going on. Hobby, music, and sports stores are filled with ideas. Recreation centers and recreation agencies are there to help. Just get the information first. Then, pick and choose. But, if you enjoy being bored, forget it.

Boredom is an old disease. In the eighteenth century, Giovanni Casanova called it "that part of Hell Dante forgot to describe."[9] Boredom is here to stay. . . . especially during leisure. It is one of the chief companions of the leisure waster.

4.

Three Fools from the Wasteland

The Fickle Funster, Disjointed Joiner, and the Focal Fool
Are all such artists at misusing time
That they manage the Wasteland School.

The Fickle Funster, Disjointed Joiner, and Focal Fool
are three types of leisure wasters that you have probably
met. While the Focal Fool can concentrate on only one
thing at a time, the Fickle Funster and the Disjointed
Joiner are going in all directions at once. They can be
complimented, however, on the intensity at which they
follow their special talents.

The Focal Fool is a slightly nearsighted fellow. He can't
see much further than the end of his nose—so he turns
the full force of his vision on what is directly in front of

him, blotting every other peripheral image completely
out of the picture.

Charlotte Buhler has presented such a perfect picture of
this type of leisure waster that it is included here:

An Example is Sanford D., 59, partner of a very competitive,
younger colleague in a legal firm of which they are co-owners.
Sanford who says of himself that as an attorney he was fairly,
but not exceedingly, successful and that in his marriage, he
was reasonably, but not altogether happy, has suffered for years
from migraine headaches and yielded finally to his doctor's
urging to seek psychotherapy.

His story is that of a hyperconscientious, perfectionistic person who keeps his nose to the grindstone of work and neglects
everything else in life. He has no sport, no church, and few
social interests. He never travels, and he seldom takes vacations
because he does not know what to do with them. When his
doctor tells him to relax and take it easy, he is at a loss to know
how to accomplish this.

"My life is dull," he says, "but I don't know how to change
it." His wife, the daughter of friends of his parents, he claims
to love, and she is the only woman he has ever slept with. She,
a rather charming and lively person, thought him "a little
stuffy" when she met him, but he appealed to her by being
more considerate and more serious-minded than the other
boys she had dated. They were fairly young when they married, and they had three boys. He did not seem to enjoy his
children, with whom he had little contact and whose noisy
games disturbed him as much as their dirty fingernails.

"I don't know what he does enjoy, except his office and his
collections," says Janet, his wife. "Most things that people enjoy, are a waste of time and money to him." When they go
out, he is a wet blanket in every group. When she tried to
take him away from his work for more than a prolonged weekend, he got quite unhappy and restless and went back to work
and worked twice as hard as before.

As the years went by, she did not feel that he loved her or
anybody. Nobody could really reach him. Yet he claimed that
all he did was work, so the family could have a nice home and
a good life. Perhaps this was true. But she preferred to have
less material and more emotional satisfactions in her married
life. Now that Sanford is older, he worries about earning and
saving enough before he retires. Yet neither he nor his wife

can see what ever else he would want to do except work. There is nothing else that has meaning for this man, and everything besides work means mostly boredom to him or gives him grounds to complain, like noisy grandchildren or chattering friends. "Every day I am glad when it is over," he said. His is a truly meaningless life.[1]

So much for the Focal Fool. His concentration smothers out all the life and leisure around him. However, he is a leisure waster cum laude.

The Fickle Funster is an interesting person. He is just the opposite of the Focal Fool. The Fickle Funster is a person who cannot stand the "old" and is forever searching for "freshness" of experience. He runs from one activity to the next, but only after investing considerable time, interest and money in each.

The equipment of a Fickle Funster would furnish any recreation center with activities for quite a period of time. His garage is filled with aqua lungs, exercise equipment, a ping pong table, an archery target with 20 unused arrows, bowling balls, camping gear for a family of ten, snow skiis, and perhaps even a 22-foot motor boat.

In 1962 the Fickle Funster took up badminton. He joined a club—the whole works. By 1963 he was bored so next he tried the square dancing scene. He got quite good at that, and ended up by going to New York to take part in a big square dance competition. By 1964 he realized that this activity involved too much practice, so he decided to go all out for foldboating. After an initial "worth while" investment in a foldboat, his wife decided that those long trips to the river just weren't worth it. He's thinking about flying now, but is quite anxious however, because his wife's last look at their financial situation told her that bankruptcy was approaching fast. He resents her for being such a wet blanket.

The Disjointed Joiner is very similar to Fickle Funster,

except that while the Funster is involved in one thing at a time, the Disjointed Joiner is engaged in several, strangely disjointed, activities.

The often frenzied Joiner may be a member of an Indian dance group, Great Books club, Ham Radioites, and a local branch of the Humane Society. In addition to this he may hold such offices as President of the Young Democrats, Vice President of the Art League, and Secretary for the Model Railroad Association. Needless to say, this fellow is going to be a little overworked at times, especially if he believes in reading, painting, and playing the guitar whenever he can get the chance to be alone. His responsibilities keep him running so fast that he rarely gets a chance to sit down and review the situation. He can usually be recognized by a harried, preoccupied expression. His eyes resemble those of a horse in a burning barn. His life has no direction because he never has time to try to organize his activities toward some meaningful goal. His philosophy of life is to experience all areas of life—again, without a pattern. He is usually too tired to absorb much of what he is "experiencing." In trying to grasp all of life, he sometimes has the feeling that he is getting nothing. His desire is for a balanced life, but the trouble is that the weights are too heavy.

One of the biggest problems of the Fickle Funster and the Disjointed Joiner is the wake of friends they leave behind with each interest they put to rest. Both types are bound to end up with a closet full of friends and acquaintances if they don't watch out. Often they find themselves so tired from endless rounds of social engagements that they feel like "Stop the world I want to get off!" They begin to wonder how they can tactfully and gently get rid of their legion of friends.

A recent *Time* Magazine article pointed out the problem of having too many friends and too little time. It suggested a few kind methods for the "weeding out of friends."

First step is the unreturned phone call. But never helps much, for Weedees tend toward tenacity, and even a prolonged series of never answered messages can produce a series of personal notes and even registered letters or telegrams.

Other methods include the Stretch-out and the Cross-up. The first consists of gradually increasing the time between engagements; if the established home-and-home rhythm for the exchange of dinners has been, say, two weeks, let four weeks go by before asking the Weedees back—and then six. The Cross-up involves preliminary groundwork. Find out when the Weedees have theatre tickets, and ask them to dinner that night. This has the added advantage of ostensibly discharging the social obligation without actually going through with it.[2]

The Focal Fool need never worry about the problem of Weedees and weeding out, for he rarely has more than a few friends. For the Disjointed Joiner and Fickle Funster it can be a real problem, this excess of friends. Another problem is the tendency for too many activities to fragmentize one's life.

Clifton Fadiman states that the solution to the dilemma of leisure does not lie in the "multiplication" of external stimuli in the area of pure diversion. More friends, more clubs, more motion is not the answer if one is going to have a modicum of the feeling that one's life is one's own. An overabundance of what Fadiman calls the "external stimuli" can organize people's lives so that they become almost powerless to direct the course of their activities.[3]

But you don't have to become a Focal Fool.

5.

The Failure to Prepare

The most dangerous threat hanging over American society is the threat of leisure . . . and those who have the least preparation for leisure will have the most of it.—ARTHUR SCHLESINGER, JR.[1]

To prepare or not to prepare. That may be the question that determines how nobly you live your leisure. One who is prepared with intellectual and emotional resources may be considered to be better off than the poor skidrow type leisurite who must grub and scrounge in off-work hours. This recreational outcast never seems to be aware of what's going on in the leisure world about him. He's unprepared to take part in anything that requires skills or training, and his attitude would kill any joy he might obtain anyway, because he feels that the only thing worthy of man is work that brings in money.

(A Roper Poll in 1957 concerning attitudes toward a possible four day week turned up the uncomfortable fact that there is not really a great eagerness for an extra day. In the Far West, a third of the respondents would use an additional day to take another job. Southerners were least able to come up with ideas about what they would do with the extra day; and do-it-yourself, hobbies, sports and trips were named less than with other groups.[2])

Another poll found that though the leaders wanted a shorter work week, the rank and file did not. In still another study eighty percent of the workers stated that they kept on working for lack of alternatives, not for positive satisfactions.[3]

Bertrand Russell advocates the cutting of working hours to a drastic four. He feels that our present age of automation does not really demand any more labor than is necessary to produce the goods of today. He worries about education however, and suggests that it be taken quite seriously:

> When I suggest that working hours should be reduced to four, I am not meaning to imply that all the remaining time should necessarily be spent in pure frivolity. I mean that four hours' work a day should entitle a man to the necessities and elementary comforts of life, and that the rest of his time should be his to use as he might see fit. It is an essential part of any social system that education should be carried further than it usually is at present, and should aim, in part, at providing tastes which would enable a man to use leisure intelligently.[4]

Actually, an education for leisure is just good sense. In present times we all are quite concerned with insurance. There are many types, covering just about any kind of calamity. Leisure can be a calamity, and can cause serious emotional wreckage. Leisure insurance is really a must and it comes in the form of classes, clubs, friends, and the literature of the philosophy and practice of leisure. Those who have such policies may not have to take the trip down to leisure skidrow when vacations, illnesses, work layoffs, weekends, times of stress, evenings, or retirement come along and tear away the under girdings of work-oriented lives.

Churchill, Roosevelt, Eisenhower, and Truman, all had a good amount of leisure insurance. They all must have realized the sustaining force of recreational interests in case of fatigue or stress. Churchill painted in oil; Roosevelt was an avid stamp collector; Eisenhower was a golf player; Truman pounded out his tensions on either pavement or piano, and rarely forgot his early morning walk before starting his daily Presidential responsibilities.

Any one who works hard and has a large amount of responsibillty needs some activity to which he can go to be re-created in terms of emotional and physical energy. Presidents certainly would fall into that category, as would business executives, housewives, college professors, and ditch diggers.

But *why* must we prepare for leisure? Why can't we just take leisure when it comes and face it as best we can? One good reason would revolve around mood. When one is bored, unhappy or in a high state of emotional tension it is a bit difficult to think of ways out of the leisure wasteland. Also, preparation in some skills (and the change of associate into friend) may take several months. It should be ready and waiting for you when leisure comes, and the individual should be able to go to it as one goes to an old friend, expecting and receiving comfort and support. It's nice to have what the hipster calls "something going for you." When you need it, it's there. The skill, friend or interest, should fit as easily as an old slipper.

The results of not planning for leisure are everywhere. We can talk about old slippers throughout this book, but the fact remains that many tired or distressed individuals pick leisure to "try wearing new shoes." Their new interests may not satisfy as a result. They haven't had time to be broken in.

Others don't even take the trouble to try something out when a period of leisure descends upon them. Many of our older citizens are feeling deserted, lonely and bored. Many housewives are finding that though they enjoy having the children in school and not underfoot all the time, all those hours in the home can become boring—even when one can drag out housework all day. The mental institutions are filled with people who failed to use leisure to relate to others but instead took trips of escape.

And how many alcoholics are there? These people certainly found something to do with leisure. They have little "emptiness" as a result of their hobby.

How many "cryers" are there? These downcasted ones find leisure time a holiday for complainers. They moan and groan about what a miserable thing life is. "Everything's such a drag!" "What's life all about? Where's a purpose?" In the days when people worked from morning to night they had little time to ask what life was all about, or to feel lonely and bored during leisure time. The shorter work week offers much more time for the "purpose paupers" to take up their hobby of moaning and groaning.

This habit of complaining just seems to be leisure "fill." It serves as a substitute for the seeking of activity outlets. Here is a case in point:

Eva L., 19, unmarried. On and off student. Eva was involved in a rather serious emotional conflict for several months. During that time her mood ran from a few manic states on down to a normal state of deep depression. She was so miserable that she decided to stay home for several months. She spent the time in reading and sleeping. Her manic states were usually experienced after some kind of "activity," usually of a recreational nature. When it was drawn to her attention that she usually returned to a normal or even happy state after her "activity" she replied that it was only natural, "after all, I have been away from my problems for awhile." When urged to engage in these activities with greater frequency Eva merely shrugged her shoulders and said that it took too much effort to get ready for, or organize them.

In her languorous state, Eva was in no condition to fight depressions. Thus she remained. A small amount of planning would have eliminated much of her "worry time." She could have arranged to meet someone for a movie or a walk. Since being with people seemed to pick her up, activities with people would be preferred to those engaged in alone. It would have taken a few minutes of arrangement, but what a difference in mental health would have resulted.

And then there's the case of the daily or recurrent mood.

Betty J., 28, married. Housewife. Every day at three o'clock Betty became so bored and listless that she wanted to fall asleep. She fought this urge because she had a habit of taking a nap for an hour at noon and so felt that it wasn't sleep that she needed. She usually drank coffee and paced nervously around the kitchen, that way killing 45 minutes until the "kids" got home from school. "I just hate that time of day" she states, "because the same old thing happens day after day. I get so bored I could scream. Maybe it's the coffee."

A little planning and organization could make this spot an enjoyable one. A hobby or interest serves as an invaluable medicine in relieving daily tired feelings or bored moods.

People are usually quite lazy when it comes to the actual recreations that they follow. But when you ask them what they would like to do in leisure, the answer is generally a more active interest. There appears to be a large discrepancy between what people actually do, and what they say they would like to do. There have been many studies that would prove this statement. One such study was that of the National Recreation Association published under the title of "The Leisure Hours of 5,000 People." Here are the results, in order of preference for activity:[5]

Did	*Would Like to Do*
1. Reading newspapers and magazines	1. Tennis
2. Listening to radio	2. Swimming
3. Going to movies	3. Boating
4. Visiting or entertaining	4. Golf
5. Reading books (fiction)	5. Camping
6. Auto riding	6. Gardening
7. Swimming	7. Playing music
8. Writing letters	8. Auto riding
9. Reading books (non fiction)	9. Theatregoing
10. Conversation	10. Ice Skating

As can be seen, eight of the ten most common leisure activities are sedentary. All but one of the activities aspired to are active. And never the twain shall meet. Perhaps the wish is larger than the energy, or the ability less developed than the interest in the activity. In either case, the fact remains that people actually engage in activities less strenuous than those they profess an interest in.

Here are some qualities of personality which send people to the leisure wasteland. These are qualities that cause them to be unprepared for leisure:

1. A negative personality
2. Lack of persistence
3. Putting things off
4. Disharmonious family or marital life
5. Lack of control over drinking, sex
6. No ambition or purpose in life beyond that involved in work
7. Insufficient education for interests
8. Bad physical or mental health
9. Inhibiting or non-stimulating friends
10. No energy, enthusiasm, or imagination
11. Shyness, inclination to avoid people
12. Feeling that hobbies are silly and interests are diversions
13. Oversensitivity to lack of perfectionism. Everything must be quality

These qualities are surefire leisure killers. They cause their "carriers" to be unprepared for leisure when it comes, and when it does come they find themselves suffering severely from pains of the leisure wasteland. Here are just a few of the "unprepared":

Martha M., 24, married, housewife. Martha states that the only thing she would really like to do is to go dancing once a week, but finds this impossible because her husband doesn't like to dance. Her husband, on the other hand, likes golf and tennis, activities which Martha refuses to learn. Both partners in this marriage have a negative attitude toward learning and participating in the activities of the other. Both feel the other is selfish and unbending. "If he won't take me dancing, I'm not about to take part in his old golf or tennis!," states Martha emphatically.

Will C., 32, unmarried, accountant. Will has a tendency to begin many things without finishing them. His lack of persistence can be seen by his enrollment at the local adult education school, and subsequent dropping of the class enrolled in. Here is a man who rarely attends a class for more than three sessions—yet every semester for the past eight years he has signed up for one or two classes. The total classes enrolled in and dropped is twenty two. The longest time he spent with a class was five weeks and that was a brush-up accounting class. "Once I get into things I find that they are not as interesting as I thought they would be," he says.

James A., 22, unmarried, filling station attendant. This is a very shy individual, who goes out for activities that do not involve people. His days spent in deep depression have recently led him to the brink of social activity. "I think I must need people because I am really too alone. I've never had friends, but I see everyone around me with other people and apparently seeming to enjoy themselves. I try to meet people but become so tense and nervous that I don't know if it's worth it. They certainly must think I'm an idiot," says James. James has a somewhat stooped appearance and mumbles when he speaks. Even his appearance is that of someone trying to escape people.

Angela H., 35, married, housewife. Angela's husband is a prominent lawyer and financially very well off. She has been troubled recently by extreme feelings of boredom which she notices also in her friends, but states that they carry on flirtations and sometimes affairs in their attempt to escape this boredom. Angela states that this sort of thing does not interest her. She says that her friends laugh whenever she suggests that she would like to take up ceramics or a few singing lessons. "They seem to feel these things are silly and wastes of time. I can't find them any worse than all the drinking and carrying on that our set does however," says Angela. "Frankly, this life is really a bore." I would love to do things that interest me, but there is always the teasing on their part. This takes some of the pleasure out of it." Angela cannot imagine herself in any other social circle, in fact she does not seem to realize that any others exist.

If any of these personality qualities are yours, and you find that they do cause you to waste a great deal of what could be more enjoyable or productive leisure, you had better hitch yourself to a pencil and paper and go to work on ideas of how you can better prepare yourself for a wiser use of your leisure time. Leisure offers great possibilities for self-development, compensation, stimulation. However, education for its use is needed. As one sociologist states:

They have no training for leisure. They have, most of them, no strong interests or devotions. The habits of their work time convey no meaning to the time of liberation. . . . Soon they too betake themselves, in their various ways, to some form of excitation. Having no recourse in themselves, they must get out of themselves. They take the easy ways out because they see no alternative. They have never learned to climb the paths leading to the pleasures that wait in the realm of ideas, in the growing revelation of the nature of things, in the treasuries of the arts, and in the rich lore of the libraries. They must seek instead the quick transport, the dream, the adventure, in the tavern or where the gamblers meet.[6]

In the *Challenge of Leisure,* Arthur Newton Pack states:

The present generation must also learn a new attitude toward activities that are non-productive in the old economic sense and in some cases even leisure activities themselves must be learned. Only by a greatly expanded educational program can all this be accomplished.[7]

Another writer speaks on behalf of education for leisure:

The fact that so many people appear to be lost or frustrated when they have leisure at their disposal shows that many have not had early experiences which would enable them to use their spare time satisfyingly. Adults whose retirement results in enforced leisure, often seem to lack the capacity for enjoying their leisure and using it a way which is satisfying to them. Thus, it may be assumed that the extent to which leisure is used as a cultural opportunity depends largely upon how well individuals are prepared for it.[8]

And yet another voice calling through the wasteland:

The trouble is, we have been training men for tasks rather than for living. When these tasks are accomplished there is nothing for them to do, and they have no personal resources upon which to draw. Education is credited with the great success and the large results accruing from these accomplished tasks; must it not also be charged with the deficiencies in the personal development of the worker?[9]

William C. Menninger, as a psychiatrist has long been concerned with mental health, and feels the same concern for an education for leisure program: "The challenge lies in the realization that training, or a lack of it, largely determines what people will do with their leisure," he states in an article in *Recreation* Magazine.[10]

Another writer adds his voice to the cacophony of voices in the battle for *interest armament* and declares that today more than ever before we need education for life and that to "enjoy leisure is to enjoy freedom. . . . We can no more afford to follow loose thinking in the sphere of leisure than in the sphere of economics."[11]

It seems that a plan is needed, and the only one to make it out is the individual. He needs to take his own "needs," financial situation and time allowance into consideration and then come up with some sort of personal leisure blueprint. It must be personal however. What is good for others may not be good for himself. He *should* have balance in his plan however, and should include some solitude, some social life and some physical activity in order to insure a certain amount of mental and physical health. His own personality would determine what degree of each of those three "health musts" he would need. Activities should be included which refresh and renew zest, energy, and interest in life. Dissipating activities should be kept to a minimum, though such activities in themselves do have a balancing value.

Planning should be fairly flexible, so that new interests that come along can be included. It should not fragmentize his life into a thousand and one different activities, turning him into a harried hobbiest or disjointed joiner. Planning should not be so intense that the planner forgets to live today. This habit of deferring gratification is a hard one to break.

This argument of a need to be educated for leisure may be summed up by an authority in the field, Martin Neumeyer:

Education for leisure is not a fad, but is essential to a well balanced program of education. If students are educated vocationally and not avocationally, the job is but half done. To be able to make a living but not to enjoy the fruits of labor means that one's preparation for life is not complete. . . . Children and adults should have interests and skills in recreation which will come to the surface when work or study tensions are removed. . . . The challenge lies in the realization that training, or the lack of it, largely determines what people will do with their leisure.[12]

6.

The People Wasters

The worst solitude is to be destitute of sincere friendship.—FRANCES BACON

Friendship, the low cost but high reward use of leisure. Why are people overlooking such an investment in time? Perhaps it is the result of the great caution about Caring that is ravenging the land. Are people loving more now but feeling it less? There would seem to be a trend in that direction. A recent *Look* Magazine article reports such a trend, declaring that it is out of fashion to "love." It is not out of fashion to experiment with sex however. The two (love and sex) shouldn't mix, according to the concensus of responses to several queries made in the writing of the previously mentioned article—which was called, incidentally, "The Twisted Age."

Erich Fromm sees the problem of love as one of more concern with *being loved* than with *loving*. He states that people are overly concerned with being lovable and work at being so by becoming more successful, more attractive, more interesting. Fromm feels that what most people mean when they use the term lovable is "a mixture between being popular and having sex appeal."[1]

What does Fromm feel is needed before one can be capable of loving? In order to love others (both in a romantic and friendship way), the individual must feel confident in his ability to accomplish a task successfully. He must have overcome complete dependency on anyone or anything else and must not be tied up with self-love. He should have faith in his own powers, and the *courage* to use his powers. He will need this courage in the art of loving and giving of himself to other people. If he lacks the courage, and is afraid to give himself, he will have a difficult time in being able to feel and give love.

What does one person give another? He gives of himself, of the most precious possession he has, he gives of his life. This does not necessarily mean that he sacrifice his life for the other —but that he gives him of that which is alive in him; he gives him of his joy, of his interest, of his understanding, of his knowledge, of his humor, of his sadness—of all expressions and manifestations of that which is alive in him.[2]

Kahlil Gibran says, "Your friend is your needs answered. . . . For you come to him with your hunger, and you seek him for peace." A friend then should answer the needs of friend.[3]

There are beautiful examples everywhere of wasteland friends who do not answer the needs of one another. For instance there are Joe and Bill, two highly dominant persons who are continually competing for leadership wherever they are. It's "King of the Mountain" every time they get together, and though the relationship is not "satisfactory" to either, they continue out of habit and the challenge of a future "win."

George, a very inactive fellow, is engaged to energetic

Betty. Neither of them are interested in the activities of the other but they feel that marriage is more than fun. They want to start a home and get down to the business of raising a family. Neither feels that their lack of interest in each others recreations is going to amount to a "hill of beans" as they put it. Such wishful thinking often overlooks the unfortunate fact that hills grow into mountains occasionally.

Consider the frictionship between Sue and Sam, two very dependent (succorant) types who need love to be given to them more than they are capable of giving it. They find their marriage a constant battle ground for whimperers. Each demands the warmth and affection of the other, while neither can give such physical demonstrations.

This entire idea of unfulfilled needs is somewhat reminiscent of Sartre's "No Exit" in which a Lesbian is after a nymphomaniac who is after a man who in turn is not at all interested in her. These miserable three are located in Hell, with the idea being that Hell is other people. It must be when each person is incapable of answering the others need that they find themselves undergoing both need and love starvation.

Friendship then, can give many things. It also means different things to different people, according to their own personality needs. In mental health, the need for social interaction has long been apparent. In this Age when there are so few psychiatrists available for a large mental hospital population, there is often as much therapy that takes place as one patient socializes with another, as there is in the actual face to face, patient to psychiatrist, relationship.

This ability to socialize is a very important factor in mental health. Menninger recognizes it as having a high recreational value:

One other prescribed recreational activity has proved, again and again, its important therapeutic value. This is the sociali-

zation provided by group activities—parties, ball games, square
dances, dramatic productions, and so on. All of us have the
desire to belong—to the family, club, gang, or to some other
preferred group. One of the conspicuous symptoms of some
types of mental maladjustment is the feeling of lonesomeness,
the inability to identify with and belong to a social unit. The
average psychiatric patient, burning his illness, is conspicu-
ously incapable of feeling comfortable with other people. An
important phase in the process of getting well is to be able
again to become sociable, and to participate pleasurably in an
activity with someone else or with many other people.[4]

Many people are devoid of the feeling that they are able
to communicate. How have we lost this ability to share, to
love? Some people may never have learned. Other people
first begin to withdraw from those around them when they
meet stressful situations and use escape mechanisms in
dealing with them rather than facing and dealing with the
actual problem. Others find that their needs have not been
satisfied in relationships with others and so have withdrawn
into a fantasy land for satisfaction, or found more realistic
satisfactions that excluded contact with people. They become purple people eaters, meaning that they avoid people
with a purple passion. They fail to realize the value of a
good friend in time of need. When problems come they
have no one with whom they could talk things over. They
have lost a valuable mental health aid—the friend. Bad
may then go to worse.

One authority in the area of dance therapy, states that
often this interaction between patient and patient in the
mental hospitals, is not a verbal one. There are various
ways to communicate and share with other people, and she
states that dance is one of them.

Whatever method a patient uses for participation with
others, whether it is singing in a group, playing instruments in
a rhythm band; or an elaborate orchestra; moving in rhythmic
action with others; or verbal conversation, it seems to afford
him an active relief to get away from feelings he experiences

while he is alone and isolated from others. The patients express themselves in these terms:

"It gives me a feeling of belonging."

"You are with the group."

"It teaches you to cooperate with others."

"I never learned to be with other people. I was never taught as an infant."[5]

How do you rate as a social personality? Are you "in" or "out" when it comes to being able to relate to other people? Take this social misfit inventory and find out.

SOCIAL MISFIT INVENTORY

(Check yes or no)

Yes No (Thank God)

I am:

Intolerant . . . .

A Rebel with a Cause . . . .

Unsympathetic and cold . . . .

A Believer in the fact that a quiet
    discussion of problems is the
    slowest way to achieve a goal

Fond of belittling type humor . .

A failure in paying emotional
    support . . . .

A loner because people are no
    damn good . . . .

Insensitive . . . .

Always right . . . .

Capable of passing up old folks
    with flat tires . . . .

Good at Nagging and talented at
    finding fault where others fail

Often called a louse . . . .

The social misfit can usually be recognized by his display of unfriendliness. One writer in the field of interaction, mentions some other characteristics. He states that they *disagree often,* showing passive rejection as well as open rejection. They also show *tension* by asking for help or withdrawing out of the field. They may show *antagonism* by deflating other's status or by defending or asserting themselves.

Helen Hall Jennings has written on the results of a study she made on the "over chosen" and the "under chosen" among a population of high school students. What were the qualities the *less chosen* seemed to have? They were:

Quarrelsome with irritable behavior
Nagging, whining, nervous

Aggressive and dominant
Attitudes which have bad effect on group moral
Rebellious
Insensitive to the group situation[6]

Not the kind of people you'd like to be in a corner with at a party. With such a coat of protective armour they need never worry about the onslaught of friendship.

What are the results of living without love? Ribble advocated that children be given large amounts of love in the form of "mothering." This consists of being held, rocked and fondled by the mother. She based her recommendations on the observations of severely neglected children, who as a result of their unloved state, had a tendency toward depression, and their bodies became emaciated. They were backward in development. Many of these children suffered from marasmus, a disease characterized by a general wasting away with no apparent organic reason. Adequate "psychological mothering" saved the day however, and the disease was conquered.[7] How many adults today suffer such a disease?

Ponder this thought about adult love needs for a moment.

To say that one will perish without love does not mean that everyone without adequate love dies. Many do, for without love the will to live is often impaired to such an extent that a person's resistance is critically lowered and death follows. But most of the time, lack of love makes people depressed, anxious and without zest for life. They remain lonely and unhappy, without friends or work they care for, their life a barren treadmill, stripped of all creative action and joy.[8]

Stop this barren treadmill, I want to get off. But do we really? Smiley Blanton, the psychiatrist responsible for the above quoted statement, states that during his first years of practice he was very much disturbed by the many people, desperately in need of love, who shied away from "even the simplest expression of understanding and sympathy." Why do they reject that which their very lives depend on their finding and accepting? Dr. Blanton answers:

It is natural to reject something that threatens one's happiness. If love has been experienced as an unhappy failure, people naturally try to avoid it. But I have seen people replace hatred with love, selfishness with kindness when they developed insight. With assistance and encouragement their true selves emerged.[9]

Many people are limited to a small circle of friends and continue with these in a longtime inbreeding of interests. They would like to meet others, make friends, learn new ways of life, but they are afraid to make the first move. They fail to realize that *every* friend was once a stranger.

People wasters are everywhere. People wasters are everywhere. People wasters are nowhere!

7.

Eat, Drink, and
Make Merry

Many a man thinks he is buying pleasure, when
he is really selling himself a slave to it.
—BENJAMIN FRANKLIN

There are several personality controllers lurking in leisure. One of these is drinking. A January 1963 *Business Week* article states that there were five million alcoholics in the United States at that time.[1] Andrew Ivy of the Institute of Scientific Studies for the Prevention of Alcoholism, claims that every year 500,000 people become alcoholics in the U.S.A.[1]

The weekend alcoholic has become a recognizable phenomena. This is not the derelict type who lives in skid row and pan handles for wine money. *Business Week* stated that only three percent of the alcoholics are of that variety. The other 97 percent are all around us, nicely dressed. These are not heavy drinkers, but genuine "vodka before breakfast" alcoholics.[1]

There are figures, figures everywhere about this drop to drink. The United States Department of Commerce reported in 1960 that 17 billion dollars had been spent on alcohol and tobacco. As a naked fact, that statement may not be too interesting, so let's relate it to something else. 1960 was a big year for school building, but build as they did (and expand and maintain) they only topped the drink and tobacco expenditure by several billion dollars.[2]

Advertising makes the difference. The ads all help form our opinions, our philosophy, even our budget. When it comes to drinking, we see that this is a very civilized activity and everyone is doing it. We see a charming family setting, or a gala party. Another full color picture features an athlete lifting high his glass while across the page we find grandma receiving a jug, the perfect Christmas gift.

Advertising tells us that drinking is the smooth, smart thing to do. It's healthful to drink now because all the rough edges have been smoothed away. And not only does this advertising sell liquor, but it inadvertently sells bad breath killers, headache pills, stomach upset medicines, and perfume.

Part of the tremendous liquor expenditures may be attributed to advertising, part to the tension relieving qualities of alcohol, and part to the fact that a glass in hand is a part of the wardrobe of anyone socializing, whether it be with friends, at cocktail parties or around the Thanksgiving turkey. Drinking is the thing to do. No one would criticize a good social cup of cheer. However, the road to nowhere is paved with good social drinking intentions. Where do people get lost, and go from social drinking to moderate drinking to heavy drinking? Many people never do, and go through life having delightful little two drink outings. Then there are the fantastiks who can do without sleep or food because they are always loaded with calories and in a state of partial sleep, all thanks to a steady supply of alcohol in the blood.

And the drinking starts young. In some teenage groups it is indeed a very fashionable thing to do. A recent coming out party in an eastern city resulted in $6,000 worth of damage, with seven of the young party goers being taken to court. Said one of the guests: "We had been drinking for two straight days, with no sleep and a liquid diet. We weren't the same people we are today. I agree that someone has a moral obligation about this damage, but I don't know who is responsible for the atmosphere that caused what happened at the party."[3]

What is the life of the true blue boozer, assuming he is a man or woman who has graduated from wild teenage drinking parties to normal social drinking of young adulthood, to moderate drinking, to an all day occupation. Is his/her life a party all the time? Or are there a few pains?

The worst pain that the true alcoholic must feel is when he is becoming sober enough to feel the chilly winds of his own life. When one's eyes are clear enough to see the disgusted face of the boss, the alarmed faces of wife and children, and the advanced face of the calendar.

It may bother the true boozer to recognize the additional lines in his face, lines that were unrecognizable in the diffused glow of alcoholic stupor. And what's that strange color in his face? What ever happened to the big, clear blue eyes? It may bother the true boozer to sense that his walk has become a little lopsided even when cold sober. He may not like the hang of his skin or the involuntary shaking of his muscles. He may fly into a rage at the tiniest whisper of one of his children. His nerves are shot and he knows it.

But all this can end in about ten minutes. Let's lift the cup and enter fantasyland, where pains are fantasy and fantasy is reality. Off we go with one great kick of the hops!

Sex is another area in which one's life may get out of control. A *Christian Century* article in 1963 predicted that in 1963 one baby out of every 20 born in the United States would be born to an unmarried mother. The same article stated that the number of births out of wedlock is nearly twice what it was in 1950 and three times what it was in 1940.[4]

Other countries are seeing the rise of sex as a leisure interest, also. One book on English leisure states that sexual intimacy in England seems to be the chief leisure resort after puberty. The middle class values of self improvement are still going strong however. An interviewer was told by one female that yes, she did sleep with young men who asked her to, but would like to find something better to do with her spare time.[5]

There are many "how to do it yourself" books out now on the subject of sex. One counselor in Texas has done it herself and seems to have developed a well organized criteria on how to enjoy the ideal sex life. If you can find her you can pay a small amount to find out just where your sexual Nirvana is. Her services are called marriage counseling I suppose, and she certainly must have changed the climate of many a marriage!

Several years ago a counselor in Los Angeles was prosecuted for advising his clients to learn more about sex. He used books, therapy and the couch. He got into trouble when he got on the couch along with a patient for a little on-the-job training.

An article in *Time* Magazine explores the fascinating far away places that lovers can arrange to meet in and rendezvous in through the fast jet services of our modern world. It's just a few minutes to anonymity and complete seclusion. The article mentions that the passport can offer a bit of a problem in that the desk clerk is usually required to collect the passport of each guest. This is handled by either taking separate rooms or "by relying on the continental savoir faire of the clerk, who checks the man's passport only and waves the lady through." This article recommends Baja California, Paris and Agistri as ideal spots for lovers who want to get away from it all.[6]

Another interesting phenomenon of our times is the "wife swapping parties" which are usually swinging affairs, if you don't mind not knowing who your partner for the evening will be until you look at the key you have fished out of the pile in the center of the host's floor. No one seems to worry too much about the neighbors in these "wife swapping" affairs because the neighbors are usually so involved themselves that to tell would be to invite their own disaster. The parties affect all classes and professions. As one woman told me: "I was surprised to find at one of these parties a very important person in our school. When I expressed surprise to another guest she merely gave me an impatient look that seemed to say that I must be terribly naive."

Upon one other occasion I was discussing the play "Who's Afraid of Virginia Woolf?" and mentioned to the professor with whom I was talking, that such a thing could never happen at——college. He gave me a look to shame any pseudo sophisticate and muttered, "What you won't know won't hurt you, but that sort of thing isn't only reserved for bohemian or arts groups you know." When I told him that I felt Albee's play just couldn't happen in an academic setting, that there would be a scandal if it were exposed, he said, "The idea of bed hopping to get ahead can go on just as well in the sacred halls of ivy as anywhere else I suppose." It started me a-wondering about how the times are a-changing.

A recent French movie called "The Lovers" offered a few sharp shocks in this area of sex and love. The story concerned a young French wife who was pretty much left alone by her hard working journalist husband. All her friends, far away in Paris, were carrying on affairs with one man after another as an anti-boredom preventative and it was suggested that she get un-bored also. The woman then proceeds to meet a polo player and have an affair that touched on only the periphery of her being. She didn't appear too excited. The affair was probably about as boring to her as the diversion of gardening would be to one who didn't care about gardening in particular. It's something like forgetting about the intrinsic values. It's as lackluster an activity as can be found in the leisure wasteland.

The following example is one stated to me by a secretary who believed in fulltime employment:

Jan L., age 26, unmarried, secretary. Jan reports that she frequently spends weekends away with her married boss. "It was exciting in the beginning because it was new, but now I find that I'm more nervous and not really sure of how I got into this," states Jan. She is concerned about her future and wonders what her mother would say were she to know. Jan feels a sense of shame, but worse than that she says she dislikes the feeling that she is being used. "After all, she has him (his wife) and he wouldn't be about to get a divorce. I'm just a convenience and I don't know if I exactly want to be this kind of a creature much longer." Jan comes from a good home, only dates her employer, and has never been inclined to drink or carry on with any of her previous boy friends. She can't quite understand how this all came about.

Several of the airlines have learned that it is not a wise idea to greet the traveling partner of an executive with a big, "How are you Mrs. Executive? Glad to see you back on——Airline. Did you enjoy your last trip?" The problem seems to be that in too many cases Mrs. Executive was *not* the woman with Mr. Executive on that previous trip.

Our morality is changing, and our age of leisure will give us ample opportunity for trying out the new codes. How much tragedy will follow in the wake of the new fun forms as mentioned here. More divorce, more unhappy or neglected children, more promiscuity, more husband and wife agreements of "no sex ties." It is something to think about, soberly and through to the outcome of your experiences in "the fast age."

8.

The Forgotten Self

It is doubtful that you can live well in leisure if you have overlooked the development of self (or "ego" as Freud would call it). To live fully without one's "self" would be a bit difficult. Just how does it feel to be in this "sefless" state? Primarily, one feels as if he or she were driven and not in control of their own life. They can be driven either to satisfy their own basic needs (sex, food, security) or to satisfy the demands of the society around them. Freud said that the healthy individual is one whose ego (self) *balanced* both basic need, and social demand. Without a nice healthy self to balance in the middle, the individual tends to feel a little off balance in one direction or another. Other psychiatrists have referred to this state of mental health as ego synthesis, normality, or feelings of adequacy.

But let's look at our fellow or gal who has failed to make the balance. What are the feelings of such a person? They may be summarized as follows:

Inadequate feelings of personal worth. The individual feels that he is considered relatively worthless and unimportant; he feels helpless and dissatisfied with his abilities.

Inadequate feelings of self-confidence. The individual feels inferior and incompetent. This feeling is not only related to particular skills or fields but may be general in nature. The individual feels especially inferior in social situations.

Inadequate feelings of security. The individual feels unloved and unwanted; he feels uncomfortable and in danger. . . . He does not feel that he belongs either at home or in his social group.

Inadequate social relationships. The individual does not get along with people. His behavior is often socially undesirable and interferes with the welfare of others. . . . He lacks social skills.

Inadequate self-understanding. The individual usually lacks knowledge and understanding of his own motives and desires. He rarely has insight into the nature and sources of his problems and difficulties. He is not sure of his capabilities, potentialities, or interests.[1]

This doesn't sound like the kind of person who likes to get up in the morning. Leisure for this waster would be just a large playground for loneliness and brooding. He would not be likely to seek others and thus have his personality reflected back to himself as a result of their reactions to him. George Herbert Mead, the sociologist who coined the term "looking glass self" has stated that from the attitudes of others toward himself, the individual creates an image of what he ought to be in order to secure love and approval. If there is too great a discrepancy between the person as he sees himself and the person as he sees others expect him to be, there will be a feeling of inadequacy and failure.

There are several other sociologists and psychologists who feel that personality cannot be studied apart from interpersonal relationships. One of these is Harry Stack Sullivan.[3] Another authority, Erik Erickson, has stated that a sense of identity is experienced as a feeling "of being at home in one's body and an assurance of recognition from those who count.[4]

So the person who has not developed his "self" is likely to feel a sort of alienation, either toward his own basic needs, or to other people. In alienating himself from other people he also is getting further away from who he is because so much of himself is the result of his interaction with this world of "others."

The deferred gratification pattern may be another activity that has aided in alienating man from himself. In working hard to achieve some goal a person may forget about satisfying his basic self and instead work hard to live up to some ideal set up by those around him. Or, he may do just the opposite, and develop some basic ability to the exclusion of people around him, putting off getting to know people until he has achieved perfection in some ability. Result: wobbly ego.

What about this thing called conformity? It certainly takes a lot of steam out of true enjoyment of leisure. If people are so concerned with what everyone else is doing they are apt to follow leisure activities that are status symbols, or activities that will not cause them to stand out.

Fromm has stated that conformity is a way to relieve the anxiety that springs from separateness. Jung has said that individuality is a delicate thing, easily intimidated. He felt that it was a very difficult thing to bring into consciousness when it had been too long controlled by conformity or society rule.[5] Paul Tillich, the theologian, states that we need *courage* to be. Fear and anxiety, says Dr. Tillich, cause us to choose "not to be" as personalities rather than affirm ourselves and thereby accept all the pain and effort that may go with such self-affirmation.[6]

Perhaps the birth of individuality is just as painful as physical birth. But as they say about birth giving, "Once it's over you're so happy with your creation that you forget the pain!" "To be or not to be" is really quite a question.

The time has come to seek one's own. The time has come to find out who we are. The time has come to become an individual. Why? Mainly because the leisure is coming that has long been coming, and without knowing *who* we are and *what* we really want to do, we will all be forced to climb the walls of the leisure wasteland.

The time has come to say things like "Now work is not going to distract me from finding out who I am. This extra leisure I've got is going to be time in which I face who I am and what I want. Come time off I'm just going to lock the doors and peek inside myself. Good grief, I hope there's something there!" Or maybe you will say revolutionary things like, "Leisure, I'm going to enjoy you and stop working in the blasted garden. I have never enjoyed working in the garden even though my wife calls it my 'hobby' and the neighbors say I'm gifted that way. I'm going to take up something I want to do . . . like wilderness camping or deep sea fishing. That's me, and I want to be me, once in a while anyway."

The time has come to choose the things you want and need in your leisure. A famous psychiatrist states that people do not choose discriminately in leisure even though they do have choices. He makes an analogy between selecting a used car and selecting a leisure activity. How careful we are in looking over the used car. We examine over, under, around, and through. Recreation "buying" is different. Oftentimes we accept the first thing that comes along. We don't look over various makes and try them on for size. Many a person collects stamps because Beulah does it, or goes hiking because Mike says it's good to stir up the legs. How many people go to concerts, ballet or opera because the crowd says it's the thing to do. All these things are good, but are they motivated by conformity or because they are true needs of the individual that yearn to be satisfied? If that would be the case there would be a great feeling of well-being following the completion of these interests. Is there?

This lack of interest in one's own needs was brought to my attention once in a hobby shop. A woman was browsing through the shelves and when asked what craft she had selected, she stated, "Oh, anything will do." It was evident that she didn't have any realization of her own needs, because not all things will do. Sometimes a person can run down an entire list of hobbies, each of which has a sad, fuzzy impact, and then all of a sudden they discover their hobby! And what a difference in enjoyment it brings. "This is it! I can get so absorbed in it that I forget everything else that's going on around me."

This discovery of "my activity" can be found in sports, reading, cultural activities and social groups. It comes when certain needs of the individual are given expression. It's too bad that this so often occurs haphazardly, or by accident. It's too bad that more people don't know their needs, don't know activities that satisfy such needs, and then procede to find "their activity." With an "anything will do" attitude the individual is merely gambling with his happiness. But then, it serves as good "time-fill." If "busy work" is needed, why bother about making it match the personality?

Hand in hand with the tendency to overlook one's needs in the selection of a recreational activity, is the tendency to forget activities that do offer strong gratification. Take for example the person who experienced a great joy at playing golf several years ago. A few things interfered for awhile and now his clubs hang in the garage, just as forgotten as all the gratification obtained from the golf game itself. What an amazing memory it is that causes people to forget joy! Maybe we forget all strong feelings and remember only the weak ones. Maybe if we remembered what joy was and what loneliness was, we would hustle a bit before allowing the unpleasantness to return and the joy to fade. Maybe our television set has tranquilized us so that neither strong pain or pleasure gets a chance to make an impression.

But what are these "needs" that are continually being referred to? I'd like to use the "needs analysis" of psychiatrist H.A. Murray. These are personality needs and vary in intensity with each individual.

PERSONALITY NEEDS

Affiliation:	To draw near and enjoyably co-operate with another. To be loyal to a friend.
Succorance:	To have one's needs gratified by the sympathetic aid of another.
Nurturance:	To give sympathy and gratify the needs of another.
Order:	To like neatness, organization and cleanliness.
Change:	To like variety and contrast. To find it difficult to keep to any routine.
Deference:	To admire and support a superior. To praise another or conform to custom.
Autonomy:	To get free, shake off restraint.
Dominance:	To control one's human environment. To enjoy commanding, persuading.
Achievement:	To accomplish something difficult.
Sentience:	To seek and enjoy sensuous impressions of sound, sight, touch, smell, movement, taste.
Exocathection:	To engage in practical, concrete action. To do rather than think.
Endocathection:	To live imaginatively. To like time alone to think and ponder.

Many people are engaged in activities that are not satisfying their own personal needs. The activities as a result are flat and unsatisfying. In some cases they even cause severe conflict within the person. Here are a few examples:

Bob B., age 42, married, salesman. Bob is a member of a group in which he has no leadership role, but is struggling to play a submissive, *deferent* role. This is hard for him to do because he is basically a strong leader. Bob is often a hindrance when he sits back and criticizes the methods of the leaders in the club. He refuses to accept a leadership role, declaring that it would involve too much responsibility. He appears to use as much energy fighting leadership as would be required were he to assume it. He seems to be trying to take a *deferent* role, and this is difficult as he can see better ways of doing things and is thus unable to support the leadership because he does not consider them capable. Bob is often tired after club meeting and often has a headache.

Susan L., age 30, married, housewife. This is a very sensitive person with delicate sensual perceptivity. Susan is happiest when oil painting, a craft at which she is very good. She has a streak of madness, however, that made her accept the presidency of a women's political group. Her writing interest got her into the group initially, and she was asked to write some human interest stories on the candidate that the group was supporting. Susan has no interest in persuasion or group control. If she is going to convince another to her point of view she would rather do it through art or literature, through some kind of a creation which expresses the way she feels about some particular matter. Before every club meeting she experiences severe stage fright complete with tight throat, weak knees and sick stomach. Susan is a *sentient* person in a role calling for a moderate degree of *dominance,* a quality she does not possess to any observable degree.

James W., age 22, unmarried, graduate student. James is a very independent sort of fellow (*autonomous*) who wanted to see Europe and so signed up with a travel group that was to live with families in European homes. James is like a fox in water and hates every minute of doing what he is not by nature inclined to do. He is constantly required to be either with a group and participate in the group activities or to be with the family and account to them for everything he is going to do (and they do not like him leaving the home too often). James wants and needs freedom. He often gets a tight choking sensation in his throat, as if he were grasping for air. He knows that it is merely his body struggling for freedom. He also realizes that he must never again get into a situation when he is totally unable to go off on his own. He does not like dependence and he does not like too much affiliation.

Wilbert P., age 40, married, machine operator. An introvert, Wilbert has always been very happy just to follow every request of those around him. Life has been good to him because he has been able to pursue an occupation that is relatively decision-free. There are few responsibilities and everything runs pretty automatically, both at work and at home. His home life has been directed by his wife. But now disaster! His wife Stella has just decided that she wants her husband to move upwards and onward and become a supervisor. She wants him to play golf and "meet a few people," and to join and become active in a plant associated political group. "And to learn how to express yourself you should get into one of these book discussion groups," she says in her review of possible ways in which Wilbert can move ahead occupationally. Wilbert feels lost. This seems to be an example of a leisure based on spouse direction and not on one's own needs. There will be little need satisfaction, except the need to satisfy his wife. "If it makes her happy," says Wilbert, putting on a weak smile. Wilbert is a highly *succorant* individual who has been thrown into an *achievement* and *exocathection* role. It is doubtful how easily his natural *deference* will allow him to assume a *dominant* role.

Each of the above four leisure wasters is living without regard to their own personal needs. They have been forced into situations or have unwittingly drifted into them, and there will undoubtedly be a great deal of conflict between *what they are* and *what they must do* in order to carry on with the activity. When one is meant to lead, it is difficult to follow completely and submissively. A sensitive, creative individual is often shocked at the "guts and thunder" of group leadership. Other people may be natural group leaders, manipulating people as easily as it is for them to breathe. People who need freedom and room to move may not appreciate the closeness of group living and activity. People who like to think and live reflectively may not appreciate having to produce something, or being forced to participate in some form of social *action*. They may feel so disinclined to action that should some event come up that they would be requested to attend, headaches may arise that will give an excuse for their not engaging in an activity that conflicts with their own personality needs.

There are examples everywhere of people who are participating in activities that are not "theirs." They do not "know thyself" and this lack of insight is responsible for the general sensation of *drifting*, or the apathetic state of never being really satisfied or happy. Other symptoms of an unsatisfied self may be:

Excessive drinking
Bitterness and complaining about everything and nothing
The feeling that life is going too fast
Headaches or other psychosomatic problems
Chronic fatigue
Boredom
Little energy
A very uninteresting personality

Here is an interesting theory about needs! It is the theory of the psychiatrist Gardner Murphy[8] and it concerns motivation—or *why* we do things. Dr. Murphy states that within each *sense organ*, or within the *muscles* of each individual person—there are *tensions*. Certain activities relieve these tensions. Whenever you find an activity that really does it, really makes you feel great, whenever this happens, you have found an activity that relieves the tension in your particular set of sense organs or muscles. It is not likely that another person would receive the same reaction to an activity that you do because it would be unlikely that the other person would have the same sensual or muscular tensions. Here is the formula:

Tensions + Activity = Tension Reduction
(Sense organ or (Swim, paint, read)
 muscle)

Let's get to some examples. One person, for instance, may get a pleasant sensation out of looking up at the stars, because a visual or kinetic (movement, blinking of the stars) sense has been gratified. Another person may have a strong sense of enjoyment at hearing an opera. He will respond because of acute auditory sense tensions that are satisfied and soothed through music.

Let's add up all the areas of muscular or sensual gratification. There are muscles throughout the body, therefore as many areas of muscle tension that the individual possesses equals the sum total of enjoyment or tension reduction that he will receive as a result of exercising those muscles. Some people have little musclar tension and thus have little satisfaction or delight from the exercise of these muscles. Other people may have strong muscle tensions of either a general nature or within certain specific muscle groups. This type of person would get intense satisfaction from the relief of a tension build-up in these muscles.

On to the senses. There are six, the auditory, visual, kinetic, olfactory, tactile and gustatory senses. Each offers satisfaction in the following:

1. Tactile: To stroke and be stroked, to enjoy the sense of touch. Also, thermal sentience, which is enjoyment of warm water, rays of sun.
2. Olfactory: Pleasurable odors, scents, perfumes.
3. Gustatory: Delicious food, sauces, desserts.
4. Auditory: Sounds of voice, music, nature, etc.
5. Visual: Pleasurable sights in light, color, shape, movement. Clothes, art, landscape.
6. Kinetic: Pleasurable muscular movements. Skating, dancing, skiing, gymnastics.

What suits the goose may repel the gander. One cannot fool his senses or muscles into thinking that they are satisfied. They either react through tension reduction, or they do not. What the gang, wife, boss or Bible wants does not make much of a difference, though it may psychologically.

Murphy feels that these drives have been built into the organism by evolution (are organic) and not by learning.

Thus, a music form may be enjoyed because it soothes or excites organic tensions, rather than because it is associated with pleasant periods spent with that type of music in childhood.

With the above statement in mind, it seems obvious that what we "should" do may not satisfy basic needs. The person that is continually doing what he "should" do is going to wonder why he never seems to be able to really enjoy anything. He never seems to be able to relax, for he "should exercise, should read a book, should play with the children, should do something creative, should socialize." He is so busy satisfying his sense of obligation that he starves his true needs to death. Needs are personal, differing with each individual, and have little to do with "shoulds."

Of course, there *are* many things we should do for a well balanced personality. First of all we should find out what our needs truly are, so that they can have a strong place in any balanced plan of action that we intend to develop for our lives. In this way we are not alienating ourselves from our basic self.

Now I would like to present a picture of a person who had overlooked self in the planning of his life's activities, and as a result, lacked an appetite and zest for life. Let's call this person Joe, and see how the need concept of Murray and the sense and muscle tension concept of Murphy, fitted into Joe's life.

Case Study

Joe L., age 24, unmarried, in business with father.
Background: Joe has always been very much directed by his parents. His father, a very successful businessman, took a great deal of time and trouble to make Joe into what he wanted Joe to be in order to take over the business at some

later date. His mother is a very sensitive and cultivated woman who shares her husbands interest in the development of their "work of art," that being their son. Joe was exposed to many cultural experiences as a child. He was taken to all the better restaurants, theatres, lectures and art shows. He was given "good" books to read and invited to take part in the many stimulating and intellectual conversations that often took place in their home, with invited guests.

Personality: Joe is somewhat unsure of himself and relies a great deal on his parents (deference). Joe enjoys intense participation in activity, both physical and intellectual. He is primarily interested in action, but has strong reflective tones running through his personality (exocathection and endocathection). He likes a variety of activity (change), is more interested in giving aid (succorance) than receiving it (nuturance) though his parents are very interested in having him receive their aid and direction. He went through quite a struggle for independence (autonomy) at one period of his life, but since then has assumed a more submissive or accepting attitude toward the desires of his parents to help in the development of his life. He enjoys landscapes, clothing and furniture (visual sentience). He likes to be around people (affiliation) and engage in discussion. He also likes to be alone (seclusion) and think about books he has read, philosophic questions, or about current events. The balance falls in favor of social life however and should it fall toward seclusion he becomes a bit morose. He must have time alone at the frequency of about two hours every four days. Then *his* needs for socializing and solitude are quite balanced.

Interests: Joe participates actively and regularly in: dining out, attending music concerts, practicing on the piano, tennis and group discussion. Of these interests, only group discussion gets a very enthusiastic response when he speaks of it.

Needs; Muscle and Sense Tensions: The activities that Joe states he would participate in "under the right conditions" and the activities that he participates in, are *not* the same. Here is a Chart where strong and weak satisfactions were noted:

Experiences

Strong Satisfaction	Little Satisfaction
Skiing (autonomy, kinetic, visual) "Feel free, have sense of power, like scenery."	Concerts (auditory) "I go because my parents love music and it pleases them and I like to see them happy."
Riding Greyhound bus (kinetic, visual) "I start thinking and it excites me to do so. I get very creative about my life and future also."	Dining out (gustatory) "I am not a real connoisseur of fine foods though my Dad would like it if I were. My idea of an interesting date with a girl is not to go to a restaurant."
Group Discussion (affiliation, endo-cathection, autonomy of ideas) "The thinking and discussion gets me very stimulated and excited."	Piano (auditory) "I don't like the sound of the piano especially. It's a cold form of music to me."
Guitar (auditory, endocathection) "Folk songs seem to have a lot to say. I like the ideas they present. The sound is regular and calming."	Plane travel (kinetic) "You become too cut off from what's going on. My parents hate my love of bus riding however."

The Problem: Joe is a very nonchalant sort of person. He seems bored and detached, though he does get excited when in an interesting conversation. He states that he is a lot happier when doing "silly, time wasting things like going skiing for a week, or taking off on a Greyhound." He keeps that to a real minimum because his parents feel that skiing is too dangerous and tennis is a much more sophisticated sport. His parents think his interest in buses is "positively ridiculous." "My parents are wonderful," states Joe. "They have done so much for me, at least I can go along with them in leisure activity." As a result of this complete submission of his own wishes, Joe has alienated his basic needs and interests from his external behavior. His ego balance is way off to the side of social control.

The Solution: Severe motivation caused Joe to change his approach to life. The motivation came in the form of a girl friend who refused to marry him because he was "too much under mommy's thumb." When Joe named the activities that gave him satisfaction and saw the difference between those and the activities he usually followed he became quite concerned. He moved out of his father's house and began to follow the activities that gave him real recreation from the tensions and pressures of his employment. He has much more energy since he has thrown the non-satisfying activities out and replaced them with things that he gets excited about. His father is not too happy, but is pleased when Joe talks about his plan to learn how to appreciate music by a half hour weekly program he has set up.

As has been mentioned before, the self has ways to make itself felt if the individual refuses to recognize it. Little energy, boredom, headaches . . . all are forms of revolt of the self. The self does not like to be forgotten.

The self will not be forgotten.

9.

The Forgotten Body

> He walked about the whole day and only brought
> back three birds, but to make up for that—he
> brought back, as he always did from shooting, an
> excellent appetite, excellent spirits, and that
> keen, intellectual mood which with him always
> accompanied violent physical exertion.
> —LEO TOLSTOY in *Anna Karenina*

How fit are you? On page 83 is a test to help you ascertain the condition of your physical system. It is to be taken in complete seriousness and morbid silence.

If you answer these questions with an abundance of yeses you are just about ready for the weekend sofa detail. It is normally a good idea to get up and move about during your leisure time, but if you fill the unfitness description it is doubtful whether you can get up without feeling like 20 miles of rough road.

"I'm going right out to buy a bar-bell set," says the suddenly flab conscious individual. "A badminton set for the back yard would be great with a ping pong table on

Question	Yes	No
Does your fat hang low, does it wobble to and fro?..	____	____
Is your posture bad with concave chest and slumping torso?	____	____
Are you constipated because of poor circulation or even poorer diet?	____	____
Are you a shallow breather with little zest?	____	____
How is your fatigue—chronic or periodical?	____	____
Is your heart tiki-taki?	____	____
Do your ulcers throb much?	____	____
Is your bladder embarrassingly weak?	____	____
Do you have a headache a day to keep happiness away?	____	____
Are your nerves keeping you a prisoner?	____	____
Does it take you a long time to unwind?	____	____
Do you get a lot of exercise tossing and turning at night?	____	____

the side. Oh yes, I'll pick up a volleyball and try to get the neighbors to become active too!"

A week or two later our hero can be seen on crutches coming out of the heart specialist's office. The doctor is saying, "The sprain in your shoulder will make it difficult for you to use those crutches, but you certainly need them after breaking your leg when the bar bell dropped on it. Too bad this mild heart attack had to complicate matters. I'd shake hands with you but the thumb sprain bandage would make that difficult."

We often forget all about our bodies. This ever-working piece of equipment that we haul around with us wherever we go gets an overlooking that would be fatal with our budgets, cars or household gadgets. We don't give it enough sleep, then at other times give it too much. Shoes are too tight, and so are belts—with the rewards going to the anti-acidity and constipation pill peddlers. We go too fast, too far and too much. We live by the pill and take pills by the piles.

By the time leisure hits us we are a physical and emotional shambles. Then we tell ourselves that we are going to enjoy some activity or another. Forget it! Go to the hospital instead. There the body will be remembered. There you will be safe. Leisure should be a time spent for getting into condition, not out of it.

What causes body breakdown? How does a general state of physical misery come about? Here are several conditions which affect resistance to disease and cause bad physical condition:

Defective function of endocrine glands, especially the cortex of the adrenal gland.
Altered body chemistry (example: decrease of Alkali reserve; increase of blood sugar; presence of alcohol in tissues).
Adverse temperature changes, especially chilling.
Overfatigue, especially when prolonged.
Chronic constitutional diseases of some types. (Example: diabetes.)
Poor circulation, from inactive habits or other causes.
Other infections already present.
Dietary deficiency of protein.
Dietary deficiency of minerals, especially of calcium.
Dietary deficiency of vitamins, especially of A, and C.
General malnutrition.[1]

"Oh I've seen all that before," you may say through a yawn. "And I'll see it again." And then you may proceed to ruin your body by completely disobeying anything that sounds like a health rule.

We may forget about the body, but the body doesn't forget about us. It has several ways of sending us messages, to tell us that it is unhappy about the way it's being treated. Adrenal glands may flood us with energy or else withhold it. Blood sugar level has its own way of making the body feel nice or not so nice. Gastric secretions of the stomach or duodenum have their own ulcerous forms of communication. The emotions may become involved and through feelings of fatigue tell us that we should rest. And then there's the activity of the autonomic system. This is a very active system and serves to either calm us down or keep us "up in the air."

The autonomic *nervous* system (for anyone who is interested, and we really had better get interested soon) is made up of two divisions. The parasympathic system handles the daily living routine of the body. The sympathetic system mobilizes the body for action. The nervous systems are just what the name implies—nerves which act together to achieve a function. As long as the nerves of the parasympathetic system are operant our lives run rather smoothly and our emotions are pretty much on an even keel. When a trouble comes along, or a tension or pressure, the sympathetic system goes into action. It gets the entire body ready to fight the problem. The retina of the eye is dilated so that the eye can see better, the cerebral arteries are contracted in order to push blood faster, the heart is accelerated to produce more blood, the contractions of the stomach are stopped and the bladder is also contracted. These last two organs are inhibited in activity for awhile so that they will not interfere in the body's mobilization action.

The general picture with all this physiological activity going on is that of Cassius Clay stepping into the boxing ring. Maybe it is also you, leaving the house for work. The sympathetic system operates to get the body ready for action, but in this day of rush and stress, the body may remain in this state for a long time. Then troubles appear.

After a period of considerable tension, due to the activity of the sympathetic system in mobilizing the body, the eyes may begin to feel strained. Headaches may appear from the unrelieved contraction of the head arteries. The stomach may not like being stopped from secreting juices when you are giving it something to eat, and the tension caused by its trying to control the disgestive action when you have forced something into it, may cause a stomach ache, cramp or ulcer. The bladder doesn't like being held in a state of tension too long either. It may lose muscle control and fail to be as patient as you would prefer it to be.

In short, without relaxation and without rest periods in between states of tension, the body tries to tell you that you are not treating it right by: eye strain, headaches, ulcers, constipation, poor bladder control, high blood pressure and a general, overall flaked out feeling.

This is how the body tells you that it wants to be remembered. It does not like being dulled with pills; loaded with tension; prodded on by unsympathetic "high-achievers"; told to mind it's D.P.G. (Deferred Gratification Pattern, or "don't relax"). The body wants to be provided with enough food and the right kind, but not too much, and not a nutritionally empty kind. It wants 8 hours of sleep, not much more and not much less. It wants "slow down" periods, solitude for thinking and people for stimulation. That last is important, for people help stir up adrenalin through their love and friendship. And last but definitely not least, the body wants EXERCISE. Every muscle, fiber and cell needs exercise. *Regular* exercise!

A director of recreation in Pasadena California, states that adults may need a recreation program more than children:

We need incentive which will get us started and retain our interest. That's why daily physical conditioning, even if it's just a few minutes a day, is necessary. People are pushing themselves emotionally, and physically they've gone to pot.
There's no easy way to get started, but you'd be surprised that once you're over the hump, physical fitness can become a habit. . . . Now the sports programs are carrying it beyond the idea of just doing pushups, chinups or deep knee bends. After a person gets in shape he can become a "member" of participating teams such as softball, bowling, tennis.[2]

Cardiologist Paul Dudley White states that as for physical exercise, the heart and blood vessels do not merely tolerate exercise, they thrive on it.[3] It must be a regular exercise however, and not strenuous if one is out of condition. A wild, overactive game of squash for someone who has been sitting in an office and before a television set for the last three years, would probably be just what the doctor *didn't* order.

Everyone seems to get something different from exercise. The voices ring out:

I become very creative and seem to do my best thinking after exercise.
I feel better all over—posture, color and alertness.
More spring in my step.
I have much more energy after exercise.
Sports people have spirit. It's enjoyable to be with them, participating in some kind of activity.
It's better than a cup of coffee for waking me up.
I can sleep better if I've exercised.
Exercise is the only way to get rid of tension.

Gene Tunney is naturally all in favor of being in good condition. It helped him through many of his in-the-ring, boxing bouts. He says it helped him live better outside the ring also. He says:

You can buy substitutes for exercise in any drugstore—headache powders, antacids, laxatives, pick-me-ups—which promise to confer priceless blessings. But you need never buy them again. . . . Today exercise is a voluntary effort that all civilized men and women should make toward physical perfection—a quickening, cleansing discipline that does for the body what prayer does for the spirit.[4]

And this exercise can take place in leisure. Take some of those extra hours and invest them in physical conditioning. The investment will pay off in livelier living in the rest of your leisure. If you're not in condition, the added leisure will just give you more time to think about how bad you feel, as you creep around the leisure wasteland. (And of course, without health, a great deal of your leisure *will* be wasted.)

Perhaps future man won't need health, however. Let's look at him. He will probably have a large head and tiny body (due to the fact that his only exercise is thinking), and will most assuredly be undersexed. His drives along sex lines will probably be quite controlled through pills; stress; or the fact that he is not too attractive physically with his shallow chest, thin legs and anemic complexion. His body will be regulated by pills and machines perhaps. Vibrator machines will rock the tensions out so he can go to sleep, activity pills will pep him up enough to make him bounce out of bed in the morning. An oxygen machine will help him breathe deeper and thus get more oxygen into each cell.

And so the forgotten body will get smaller and smaller, while the mind that forgets it grows larger and larger.

10.

Fatal Fatigue

Oh, so fatal to fun, is fatigue!

Many people today are tired to death. They are tired to the death of their leisure enjoyment. How many doctors are hearing the same old complaint? "I don't know why, but I'm always tired! Sleep can do nothing because when I wake up I'm just as tired as when I laid down. The truth of it is, when I lie down, I can't fall asleep. How do you like that? Here I am, oh so tired, and I can't go to sleep! It's ridiculous!"

Fatigue comes in two forms. *Objective* fatigue arises when the body is just too tired to go on. *Subjective* fatigue appears when you do not feel inclined to go on. This lack of inclination to continue in an activity can come from boredom, fear, conflicts or frustration. Both objective and subjective fatigue are effective in calling bodily activities to a halt.

E.J. Kepler,[1] an authority on fatigue and a doctor at the

Mayo Clinic, has had a great deal to say about this subject of being tired. Dr. Kepler believes that the modern way of life is ill-adapted to our bodies. Chronic fatigue rarely afflicts individuals who work with their muscles, and Kepler feels that it tends to be a disease of the intelligentsia. These intelligentsia do not have to be highly educated individuals. Thus Kepler feels that chronic fatigue is more psychological than physical. He states another interesting fact. Kepler says that the chronic fatigue occurs most frequently in early childhood and in old age. These are periods when people are looking ahead to what they would like to achieve, and looking back on what they have or haven't achieved. He then suggests that if more people could learn to live within their limitations there would be less chronic fatigue.

Whatever is said about fatigue, one thing is certain: Fatigue is unpleasant. It is one of our most deceptive feelings, for though we feel tired and want to rest, moderate physical activity usually will eliminate the feeling of fatigue. We must learn to doubt the great deceiver fatigue, and ask ourselves what the tired feeling is actually trying to tell us.

Much has been written about fatigue. If it is a problem of an age where there is too little emphasis on physical exertion, as Kepler states, then we should be in for a great increase in sensations of fatigue. If, as some experts state, it follows periods of uncertainty and stress, we can be sure that there will be much more of it as our stress count goes up.

But just what is this feeling of fatigue trying to tell us? Let's ask the experts:

Fatigue follows prolonged exertion and requires rest, preferably sleep . . . But fatigue itself is in turn partially dependent upon motivation. Boring tasks tire one much more quickly than interesting activities. We may play tennis for hours, but a half hour spent in weeding the garden leaves us exhausted.
—R. W. HUSBAND[2]

Fatigue is a general sensation, which is felt in the muscles and joints all over the body. It is believed to be due to the accumulation of waste products in the blood.—F. L. GOODENOUGH[3]

Relative fatigue, then, is not a mere limitation of human efficiency. It is not exhaustion, but prevents it. It is a conservator of organic equilibrium . . . The incapacity of the young child for long-continued monotonous tasks may be a symptom of an active, developing mind.—R. DODGE[4]

Fatigue may be traced down in the end to the sources of energy . . . There is no fatigue as long as a purpose itself is not fatigued.—R. B. CATTELL[5]

Let's add all this up. We have three opinions on how fatigue is caused. Both Husband and Cattell state that it is caused by lack of purpose or interest in a task. Goodenough suggests that waste products in the blood are the cause of fatigue, while Dodge feels that it aids in preventing the person from getting *really* tired.

Many authorities on fatigue state that in our present Day and Age psychological fatigue is much more common than is physiological. In fact, they feel the changes of people today for working hard enough physically to get tired, are much more rare than they were when hard labor was more common. These waste products that Goodenough talks about may be the cause of fatigue in cases where the individual has really done a bit of work, using great amounts of energy. Waste products in the blood are not apt to come about as a result of the activity that most of us put forth today however. Most of our fatigue of today is not caused by waste products in the blood.

The use of fatigue as a preventive of a more serious fatigue is a theory that would hold true when people are involved in strenuous intellectual or emotional tasks. Dodge has an interesting idea here, and suggests that fatigue acts as a balancing agent, causing people to stop an activity when they have reached a certain saturation point and then be able to switch to another activity until balance is restored.

The interest and purpose deficiency theory is the one that would get the most votes if you were to ask people to name the reasons for their fatigue. With so many articles out on boredom, the public is becoming educated as to what boredom is and how it causes feelings of fatigue.

A causative factor in fatigue that is generally overlooked, is that of conflict. Cattell states that smooth mental work, performed automatically and without much decision making, is relatively free from fatigue. Creative work, he suggests, causes a great deal of fatigue as it involves a certain amount of conflict in the juggling with ideas and arranging of facts or feelings.

Whenever we have to come to some kind of a decision between two or more alternatives, there is apt to be a mental exercise that may leave us fatigued. The conflict of these two alternatives uses up a great deal of energy in being resolved.

For example: Fifty words were chosen from the standard word association tests and were stated to each of the 38 women subjects. The subjects were told to respond to each stimulus word by judging it "pleasant," "unpleasant," "indifferent," or "mixed." The "mixed" responses were supposed to represent conflict, because they indicated the presence of both pleasant and unpleasant states within the individual.

The result? It was found that "mixed" judgements were the fewest and required the largest reaction times. Also, this response was accompanied by the highest galvanic skin response. (The galvanic skin response is the measurement of *tension* within the body by the aid of a machine known as the galvanometer.)[6]

Frustration has mistakenly been taken for conflict on many occasions, but the two actually are not the same.

They both cause fatigue, but that is where the similarity ends. Conflict arises when one is forced to make a decision between two alternatives. Frustration occurs whenever the person meets an insurmountable obstacle directly in the path of a goal he wishes to reach.

Frustration can range from a mild craving for some goal that is blocked, to a really traumatic experience because of the unavailability of the object desired. There are many examples of frustration-caused fatigue in the leisure wasteland.

Peggy W., age 35, married, housewife. This is a mother of four children who complains of being tired most of the time. Her children are all in school, but it is when they come home that she begins to feel fatigued. She is a fastidious housekeeper and it takes her until two o'clock every day before her housework is done. It is at this time that she would like to relax and take up some of the interests that she is so fond of. Before she was married she was an avid oil painter and sculptor. She also liked to attend the art shows and read about art and artists. She finds it impossible to concentrate on her work with the children around, stating that she needs quiet so that she can plan whatever she is creating. Result? When her children come home she gets so tired that she wants to go to bed.

Walter H., age 64, married, retired. Walter's problem is that he has very little money. He has many interests, and they do not cost very much, but he feels a sense of guilt when he asks his wife for some of their "very scarce" money, so that he can go and buy some balsa wood for a model he is working on. He gets intense satisfaction from this activity, but lack of funds frustrate him in ever really engaging in it as much as he would like to. He is often tired.

Betty J., age 20, unmarried, student. Betty is of average intelligence but finds that she has to study hard to get good grades. She has to study almost all the time, and as she is a very sociable girl, she is frustrated quite often. When there is an active week end coming up and Betty knows that she must study, great waves of fatigue come on as she sits at her desk. She can't understand why she gets so tired when she has studying to do on these weekends.

All of the above people are frustrated. All experience feelings of fatigue often, and usually at the point where the frustration occurs. When the insurmountable obstacle can't be overcome, it just seems easier to go to sleep and forget about the struggle. Others find other ways to escape from the frustrating situation. Drinking and tranquilizers are two such ways. Picking on others sometimes helps to drum out the feeling of frustration and fatigue. Then there is daydreaming, complaining, repressing and running away from it all.

Kepler has stated that chronic fatigue is most prevalent in early childhood and old age. Perhaps this is due to the frustration element found to be especially intense at those two periods of life. That fatigue is experienced more in early years may be due to the fact that one's ambitions meet many obstacles in those years. The young person feels frustrated in his attempt to be treated as an adult. There seem to be so many things that stop him from doing what he would like to do, when he would like to do it. In old age, the fatigue may be the result of any failure to achieve one's former ambitions. The fact that time has run out may be very frustrating, and may be experienced as an insurmountable obstacle preventing the chance of ever achieving one's dreams.

Feelings of fatigue have become quite widespread. They are given special exercise during leisure. This may be because in leisure (of some people) there is a lack of interest in what one is doing; or a conflict about whether one should relax, engage in some recreation, or find some work to do; or frustration over not being able to use leisure as one would like to. And the next thing you know, you're tired.

Here are a few everyday observations about fatigue. They may help you to understand the monster better.

1. The individual sometimes feels extremely tired without having exerted himself. (Example: The week end sofa enthusiast who begins to feel tired and irritable after an excessive amount of rest and sleep.)

2. Following a day of active sport, the individual sometimes would rather go dancing than rest.

3. The individual may find that his fatigue disappears abruptly if something interesting suddenly comes up. (The new interest causes a release of *adrenalin,* an activity aid which is usually produced when there is a goal to be met.)

4. If the individual once felt tired in a given situation, he is likely to feel tired again when a similar situation occurs. (Example: The man who returns home night after night and as soon as he opens the front door he feels fatigued. He may not have had a difficult day, but the habit of fatigue may be so strong, that home returning after work just *automatically* produces that feeling of fatigue.)

5. When the individual is tired, he is not likely to feel enthusiastic about anything, and when he is enthusiastic he hardly ever feels tired.

6. When the individual finds himself in an emergency situation he is able to expend an amazing amount of energy without feeling fatigued.

7. For some individuals, focusing on one object or activity with all one's energies, is a situation that calls for both intense and long lasting energy, but the individual finds himself more relaxed or excited when done, rather than fatigued.

Consider Edison and his work-filled nights and days. It is said that he required very little sleep and yet showed little evidence of fatigue. He was always interested in something and his life was filled with purpose. All his attention was focused on one subject, thereby eliminating conflicting interests. Perhaps this one of the great values of a *strong* interest in something—conflicts are pushed away and never have a chance to drain the person's energies.

Whether it be stamp collecting, oil painting or learning a square dance; where there is concentration, there is a peace of mind that comes from this unification of attention. One can be quite contented by focusing one's energies on a single object.

"But enough of all this talk about fatigue," you may say. "Aren't you making something of a monster out of a little thing?" Fatigue is a monster, I would add. And it is not a little thing.

A report on fatigue appeared in an eastern medical journal several years ago, and it showed fatigue to be a real source of concern to 240 people.[7] The findings in 300 cases, in which the chief complaint was weakness or fatigue, were analyzed. The results showed that nervous conditions accounted for 80 percent of the fatigue in those cases. These nervous conditions ranged from mild fatigue to crronic nervous exhaustion. Naturally, all other shades of "that old tired feeling" fell somewhere between these two poles. The fact that 240 people felt so bad that they sought medical attention for fatigue, would seem to indicate that it probably ranks quite high on the list of reasons why people consult doctors.

Fatigue is a very personal thing, however. It is related to one's own physical condition, emotions, conflicts, frustrations and interests. As a result, fatigue thresholds are much lower in some people than others. One person may become fatigued from the monotony of typing all day, another from reading two pages of poetry. One person may feel quite weary after a day of trying decisions, another may be completely exhausted after trying to adjust to a new job.

Fatigue is a natural enemy to participation. It is an energy stealer. It is one route into the leisure wasteland.

11.

Balancing Bunglers

One of the main problems of the leisure wasteland is imbalance. A lounging time is fine. Drinking and sex are approved also. Time killing is an occasional necessary evil. All have their place in life unless one is to live the diligent and austere life of the monk.

The trouble is, these things just aren't properly balanced. We drink, and drinking makes us forget that there is anything else in this world. We lounge and our bodies lose all enthusiasm for getting us up and dragging us around. We discover love and then procede to exploit sex in such a fashion that we use up *all* that high grade fuel that would enable us to accomplish things under full steam. Can you imagine the drive of a football player who had just spent the last two days in a happy sex life?

We focus on one activity and ride it to death. Drinkers, loungers and lovers have found a great relaxing force. They find it so pleasant that they procede to keep on enjoying and relaxing. They have found more than a tension breaker, they have found an opiate. They may never balance their lives.

A mother will cancel her child's plans to have his eighth dish of ice cream. Who is the cancellation figure in the life of the affluent adult? Is it his own inner controls? After the tranquillizing of liquor, the lethargy of a lazy day, or the exhaustion of sex—who has any controls in operation? Then may come the call for mother. Where is someone to stop us, to help us? (The poorer folks have no worry here for they don't have enough money to buy all the ice cream they can eat.)

Freud was a great believer in balance for good mental health. His ego stood for mother, even guiding us in a balance between the gratification of our basic needs and the demands of the society around us. Hopefully, mother has transferred her own control over us to our physical and emotional forms. As adults, we should be able to balance needs and society in a manner so that both are satisfied. Then we are living in a psychologically and sociologically healthy manner—according to Freud.

But what happens when we ignore one side of our ego balance? People who tend to ignore basic needs may find themselves either very tired from trying to keep them down, or overloaded from a nervous energy because they cannot find an outlet for all the drive.

Another kind of person may constantly indulge in any basic need satisfaction. He may ignore the demands of society completely. This may take the form of poor social manners. He is the character who at a dinner party, where dinner is slow in being served, may shout out "Come on, let's get it on the table!" He is very much concerned with the satisfaction of his own needs. Our "dominated by others" type character may starve to death before he would complain about the slowness of dinner. He will completely suppress his own needs because he may feel that society would disapprove should he express them.

Where is Ego, our executive in the middle? Why isn't he at the controls, seeing that we receive the best from both our self and social natures? Why isn't he doing his balancing act? In some people this Ego strongman just hasn't been sufficiently developed. So they go to one extreme or another, totally ignoring the fact that there is anything else. Some people never admit that there is such a thing as "needs," others will never admit that society or people exert any kind of control over one's life.

The balance idea goes way back in history. Aristotle[1] expressed this idea in his concept of the "golden mean" or moderation. He felt that reason seeks the balanced course between too much and too little. "Nothing overmuch" is the counsel of sanity. Aristotle did not believe in extreme repression or excessive indulgence, but did believe in the good life as consisting of a balance somewhere in the middle.

Plato[2] also divided the nature of man into three parts that needed balance in order for man to live the most fulfilling life. He said that man had a rational, a feeling and a desiring nature. The rational part was similar to Freud's Ego, and its function was to rule the body. The feeling part is one whose function is concerned with other people and actions or attitudes in relation to them. The desiring part is similar to the basic needs or ID as Freud would call it. When all three parts operate in harmony there is peace, said Plato.

Of the balance of activity, Plato also had something to say. The child should have training in both music and athletics. Music lends grace and health to the soul and body, but too much music is as dangerous as too much athletics. A pure athlete is nearly a savage and to be only a musician is to be "melted and softened beyond what is good." The two must be balanced.

Bacon[3] felt that man should become as accustomed to excesses as to restraints. He felt that the Stoic repression of desire was injurious to health and dealt a death blow to happiness. What is the use of prolonging a life which apathy has turned into premature death? Bacon also felt that it was ridiculous to control oneself too much because one's needs will appear in some form or another, no matter how hard we try to keep them down. In his essays he says:

> Nature is often hidden; sometimes overcome; seldom extinguished. . . . But let not a man trust his victory over his nature too far; for nature will lay buried a great time, and yet revive upon the occasion or temptation.

Charles Darwin felt that there are some needs that you can extinguish, however. He felt that a neglect of these needs or abilities can kill them:

> If I had my life to live over again, I would have made it a rule to read some poetry and listen to some music at least once a week; for perhaps the parts of my brain now atrophied would would thus have been kept alive through use. The loss of these tastes is a loss of happiness . . .[4]

In *Leisure—a National Issue,* Lindeman mentions the tendency to overwork one area of our lives to the neglect of others, thus causing an imbalance:

> Beginning with the organism, it becomes more evident each day that work for a large proportion of our population can no longer furnish individuals with opportunities for balanced growth and development. Millions of modern workers do their work sitting on chairs, or operating machines which require the use of the accessory muscles of the forearm and fingers and occasionally one foot. . . . Wherever machines . . . enter our work life, the obvious consequence is that the whole organism is employed to a lesser degree.[5]

It is in leisure that we may rebalance this organic imbalance that Lindeman speaks of. Other muscles, talents, abilities and needs must be given a chance to have a bit of exercise.

There are recreation philosophers all over the place who will speak up for a "balance of activity." One such writer is Jay B. Nash,[6] a man very much concerned with the need for a balance between activity and rest. He uses the term "glide-stroke" to explain his theory, stating that many people do not relax between the vigorous strokes of life. They hold themselves under high tension when they should "glide." The continual "strokers" may end up with a stroke, but of another nature.

Other writers are concerned with the possibility of too much "glide" in the choice of leisure activity. There has been an enormous increase in such passive or spectator activities as reading magazines, riding in automobiles, going to the movies, and watching television. The craving for entertainment seems to be deeply rooted in man's nature. Given more leisure, how many people would just sit . . . and watch? Given more time, would more people become tube watchers? There are many who feel that it would take a very strong counter attraction to draw people away from their television sets.

Let's get to some of the areas where balancing of activity is needed. There have been many words and thoughts expressed along this line. Here is one idea by Romney:

> Recreation as I am discussing it is the satisfaction of human hungers, just as real as the appetites for food and sex and security. . . . A hunger for self-expression and creativity, for belonging to the group and being wanted, for recognition, for competition, for adventure and for combat, appetites which exist to a greater or minor degree in every normal human being.[7]

Pullias[8] suggests the following needs:

A. To be active
B. To be with one's fellows

C. To achieve a goal
D. To overcome obstacles
E. To be creative
F. To share beauty

Pullias feel that these needs can be satisfied in recreation, and agrees with many psychologists in the belief that the greatest value of recreation is in its "wholizing" effects. The individual has needs and appetites satisfied through recreation, though these recreations should be "personalized" and designed to satisfy any particular deficiency of needs in his own life.

When recreation "wholizes" it helps the individual to concentrate on some particular activity to such an extent that conflicting tensions are eliminated. There is a sense of personality integration or unification. The absorption in the recreational activity may make one feel completely "alive" or "full of energy" for the duration of the activity, and its effects may last long after the activity. This occurs only when there is a complete focus on the activity, whether it be group singing, folk dancing, Watusing, oil painting or stamp collecting. Mental institutions have long been aware of the value of forgetting ones self through an interesting activity. Recreation acts as a diversion from the more crucial or threatening aspects of living. Through it an individual can relax some of the vital tensions and engage in a few less dangerous tensions. This relief from the more serious tensions of life may help him to see himself in a different light, get a different perspective on his life, become a totally functioning personality, or help him get closer to his basic self rather than the social-vocational figure that he exists as in the business world.

What are some of the other ways in which recreation helps to balance the overall living experience? Slavson[9] mentions the following in his book *Recreation and the Total Personality*.

Recreation offers:

A Complimentary Experience—Recreation offers balance by stimulating areas of the personality that have not been in use during occupation hours.

Discharge for Aggressive Drives—Through active sports and games recreation helps relieve pent-up tensions and drives.

Some Regressive Outlets—Through recreation one can escape from maturity for awhile and perhaps engage in behavior that might be considered childish if performed in the work-a-day world. This allows for freedom from inhibitions for awhile.

Escape from Reality—Recreation offers a respite from tensions through a sport, hobby, or interest that one can become lost in.

Satisfaction of Social Hunger—One of the major tasks of recreation is to socialize the individual, for through pleasureable experience with others his disposition towards them becomes more accepting and friendly.

Resources for Solitude—Recreation should provide some inner resources that allows the person to live with himself, alone, part of the time.

If left alone the body will work to balance any physical problem that may come along. This is not always the case with psychological deficiencies. Perhaps this is because we *force* ourselves to do so many things that the mind becomes confused and forgets *real* needs. It has repressed so much for so long it can't tell "oughts" from "needs." We become ruled by the "ought" and are constantly asking ourselves "What ought I to do?" rather than "Why do I feel this way?"

For example, consider the man who feels like he ought

to do some "home" work, but can't escape the feeling that he would really like to get together with the crowd and go out to dinner. Then there is the woman who feels that she would like to get some kind of exercise, but can't possibly imagine what or where she could do it, so she picks up the latest news magazine that she "ought" to read and proceeds to read and itch for the next hour and a half.

Then there are other times when we may feel a childish, silly kind of mood coming on but instead of experiencing it, we may pull ourselves up to full "adult" stature and become sober to an extreme—or we may go to the opposite extreme and indulge our childish whims by going on a two day binge. Both of these are examples of a lack of ability to cope with a "need" that is usually just passing by, but would like some kind of expression.

We can overlook this signaling of the mind and body. When we do so continually, we can experience some rather unpleasant feelings. Aggressive drives, for instance, when not given an outlet can dig a tremendous hole into one's soft and innocent stomach lining. A constant facing of REALITY without relief can make the nerves as jittery as a "cat on a hot tin roof."

Where is that natural sense of balance? The body has it, but why doesn't the personality come through with the same batting average. Maybe we need to put aside *everything we are taught* upon occasion, and sincerely inspect our *actual* feelings. We might try to forget occasionally about being approved by mother, *Good Housekeeping* and Reverend Goodenough, and ask ourselves, "What is this feeling trying to tell me?" Only then will you be in a position to find out if what you need at the moment is solitude, activity or people.

Perhaps some of our tensions, anxiety and personality disturbances are due to the fact that we are not flexible enough in dealing with changing living conditions. As times change, certain satisfactions are left behind and replacements are often neglected. The result is a feeling of "lack."

One example would be that of the family in pre-television days. There was probably more participation together at that period through such activities as talking around the fire or on the porch in the summer, home table games, or family piano playing and singing. The children may have been the center of attention then, rather than the television, and perhaps their antics were just as much appreciated and applauded as those antics of a Milton Berle or Joey Bishop. Today, an individual sitting around the television set may be filled with a certain uneasiness that he can't quite explain. It may seem to him that they (his family) all seem to be living in their own little world, and never really do anything in a face to face relationship. It's always "tube time."

Let's take the Sunday afternoon walk in the days before the automobile. Here people had a first hand opportunity to meet their neighbors and exercise their legs. The equivalent of this today is to turn on the television when one wants people and to go for a drive in the car when one feels the need to "get out." And so Sunday afternoon has become a bit of a drag to many.

Do we have new fulfillments for these old needs? And are these old needs still in existence? Certainly the need to be with other people, to move the muscles, to experience first hand, are needs that have always been around. The psychiatrist, Carl Jung, would call such needs archetypal. He states that "human knowledge consists essentially in the constant adaptation of the primordial patterns of ideas that were given us a priori." These primordial needs that were given to man from the very beginning are needs that man must fit into each new era, into each new environment. If he leaves them behind, strange things begin happening. He feels at a loss, and indeed he is. He is alienating himself from something that is basic within him, just because the old activity that satisfied some basic need, seems to have no place in his new life. So the activity gets junked and the individual, being unaware of the need that was satisfied through this activity, feels an undefined lack.

Erich Fromm is another psychiatrist who is also concerned with man's alienation from his basic needs. Schneider and Lysgaar, the two sociologists of "deferred gratification pattern" fame, also see man as getting away from these needs and putting off any that may send up a call to be satisfied.

To quote Jung again:

> If the flow of instinctive dynamism (energy) into our life is to be maintained, as is absolutely necessary for our existence, then it is imperative that we remold these archetypal forms into ideas which are adequate to the challenge of the present.[10]

How many old satisfactions have you remolded lately? Or do you enjoy that feeling of deficiency? Or does your fast car, loud television and cool liquor soothe any feeling of unpleasantness that may rise to the surface?

There are thousands of examples of a bad balance of activity. Look around—you'll see balance bunglers everywhere. They appear driven and tense. They may frequently be heard to ask "What is life all about?" They may complain that they never seem to feel "good." Here are a few such bunglers:

> Bill J., age 41, married, lawyer. Bill has to buy. He has just about everything money can buy and is beginning to be a little anxious because he feels that there is not too much to look forward to in the way of buying things. In developing his material stockpile he has left out the development of his personality and so while his closets and garage are loaded, his heart and mind are empty.

Jim L., age 22, unmarried, student. This student is making straight A in chemistry and failing leisure. After hours of study his idea of recreation is to pick up a magazine. If he feels really tense and "odd" he sometimes runs off and does something wild and tension relieving. He may ruin his reputation doing so, but he restores his emotional balance. All the benefits of this "balancing" activity will go down the drain as soon as he realizes that he has to face the social consequences of his act. Someday, when he is forced to pay for the window that he has just hurled a bottle through, or when some girl demands that she marry him, Jim may wonder why he never learned how to play a good, fast, tension relieving game of tennis. His activities are now only balanced when he reaches the desperate stage and then they are balanced in a socially unapproved fashion.

John J., age 34, married, gardener. This is an interesting case of a dull life. John is a gardener whose wife is very proud of their own beautifully landscaped home. After gardening all week vocationally, John's wife makes sure that his leisure time is filled with making their flower beds as attractive as those of the neighbors. John has little enthusiam about anything and seems to feel that life is just a bowl of flowers. In his case there is no balance, all his activity is pretty much of the same quality.

Joanie W., age 24, unmarried, typist. After typing all day Joanie goes home and crawls immediately into bed. "Typing is so boring I could scream" she declares, adding that she is too tired after work to do anything else. Since she hates her work and sleeps through her leisure, Joanie seems to have no life at all.

William W., age 54, married, executive. William is an executive who seems to be executing himself. His responsibilities involve so much stress and tension that he wants no more activity after five P.M. He goes home, screams at anyone who talks to him. After dinner he remains seated at the television set for six hours of viewing sedation, wearing an expression on his face that would make him unrecognizable to anyone at the office. After he feels tired enough, he heads for bed to find that all his joints are jumpin' and he can't sleep. This balance is all off mainly because William feels that it is "activity" that he needs an escape from, rather than realizing that he needs a "different" kind of activity. Then he could restore his balance enough to sleep at night.

Jane and Jim N., age 26, married, housewife and post office clerk. The N's seem to be acting just like bugs that fly into lights, thereby burning their wings off and destroying themselves. They do this same type of thing every time they run to pick up their small baby who seems to be continually afflicted with colic. The result is a crying, irritable baby and two very overly nervous parents whose nervous systems are screaming for a few relaxed moments away from their much loved bundle of responsibility. They are like the bugs in that they are destroying their normally pleasant dispositions by refusing to let a baby sitter take over for a few hours every now and then. Their lives have very little balance and are usually filled with the highest degree of tension.

Juni W., age 31, married, housewife. Juni is a prestige seeker. Every activity that Juni engages in has status attached. If it's low on the prestige point list Juni forgets it. She finds that she is always working. "I like to give large garden parties in the summer and cocktail parties in the winter. I belong to a sorority and I work actively with the better civic organizations. But don't call this leisure. It's more important. Actually, I don't have any leisure, whatever that word means."

All of these cases are examples of an imbalance in the overall living experience. We have too much of one thing and too little of another. Just as the diet needs to be balanced, so do the varied activities of life. It is in leisure when we are free to do what we want; free to balance our emotional budgets. We must be aware of where we are off balance however.

In the aforementioned cases it is doubtful if there was any understanding of where the imbalance was. Most just knew they felt "bad" most of the time. An individual cannot let the imbalance go on and expect to be able to rave about his great off-work hours and days. But how does the individual find out where there is too much monotony, conflict, zestlessness, or "other-directed" activities?

First, he must be able to take an objective look at himself. He must see what is really satisfying in his life and what isn't. He must be able to separate the wheat from the chaff. This is not easy to do. Habit is very strong in most of us and to question why we do certain things often excites a defensive reaction. When we look at ourselves defensively we must be aware that we are not seeing truth, but are seeing what we *want* to see. Objective looking is not defensive looking.

Imbalance can be caused by many things. It can occur when we neglect our personality growth in order to build up a career or pile up material products. Imbalance can occur when we do not have a variety of work and leisure activities, or if we force ourselves to engage in activities that are monotonous. We lose our emotional balance when we are lonely too much in our lives, or socialize too much. Then there is the imbalance from sacrificing everything we want so that we can get along with those around us, or if we live our lives to impress others.

Most balance bunglers could be happier with just a few tiny changes. In many cases recreation is like a seasoning. You don't need much of this seasoning, but life is pretty bland without it. The possession stockpiler could turn a little of his attention to investing some of the money he feels he must spend, into the development of a few skills. Or he could save the money and spend the time—on himself. The wild student could put a little more of his intensity into ice hockey. The day and night gardener could get up from his knees in the garden and stand up to his wife, telling her that he wants to hang up his hoe and go to the mountains every weekend with a banjo club he'd like to join. The chemistry grind could forget about reading the magazines and balance the physiological needs of his body by getting a little exercise. The typed-out typist could return to life by meeting a few people on the job and socializing for some of her tedious eight hours, thereby keeping enough light alive in her body to enable her to attend a

young adults dance group. The prestige seeker is too preoccupied with society and not enough aware that she has
her own personal self. This type is a bit like a movie set,
when you look behind it nothing is there except a few props
holding the facade up.

People do not yet realize the full importance of leisure.
Here is a great stretch of time that can be used to make
problems worse by giving them more time to take center
stage. Or, it could be invested. Planning may be required.
"Spur of the moment" activities ought to be allowed. Whatever it is, leisure activity should be personal. It should
fit YOU. Then and only then will the balance bunglers
approach the fulcrum on the balance board of life.

12.

Sadness at the Sink

Mid pleasures and palaces though we may roam,
Be it ever so humble, there's no place like home;
A charm from the sky seems to hallow us there,
Which, seek through the world, is ne'er met with
elsewhere.—JOHN HOWARD PAYNE[1]

Let's turn to the housewife, whose telephone bills, headaches, chronic worrying, nervous tension and two-hour
coffee breaks are offering some proof of a lack of self-
development opportunities. Many are beginning to question "Who am I?" Betty Friedan[2] has presented a picture
of woman in search of herself in *The Feminine Mystique*.
She states that women are finding it increasingly difficult
to ignore that voice from within that tells them they want
something in addition to their wonderful husband, children,
and home. Recreation has come up with a few suggestions
for many of these women. But more suggestions are needed
so that there may be a choice based on personal *needs* and
not just a forced choice from a narrow field because the

housewife has found it necessary to get away . . . anywhere.

Her searching for self has led her from the sink to the bowling alley complete with its color, warmth, noise, built-in friendships, and free baby sitting service. Daytime bowling is booming and it is the housewife who is keeping the ball rolling. She wants out of the house and the bowling alleys have been sharp enough to realize that their advertising must appeal to the needs of these women. They advertise that the children can have a happy time playing with an interested "teacher" while mother can relieve daily tensions, get some good physical exercise and get away from home for awhile. Mama feels quite justified in her new found interest. Bowling itself may not be so interesting to her, but what else offers so many fringe benefits?

Recreation centers have also been hearing from the housewife. Here are some typical comments made by women who have "found" the active sports and "Slim and Trim" programs that many recreation centers are now featuring.

It's about time that the recreation center started some physical activities for women. For years I've wanted to join some active group of housewives that would like badminton or volley ball. There have been others like me. The attendance at this "Slim and Trim" program proves that.

Why are there so many activities at these centers for children? Think of the time that the housewife has in her day when she could get away from the house and be out doing something with others. A recreation center should have things going all day. The morning could be for the housewife, the afternoon for the children and there should be things planned for the evening when people who work full time could get a little exercise.

This class has been wonderful for me. I'm sleeping better, have more interest in everything going on around me. I find my mind seems to go faster. I think exercise increases mental health also.

The physical activity lover is a certain type of woman whose own particular physical make-up and personality structure finds active exercise both relaxing and exhilarating. Other women may get the same sense of relaxation and stimulation in a craft club, while others may return from an afternoon session with the mother's choir feeling that singing is the greatest activity in the world. Muscle tensions, sense tensions and other differences in biological and psychological systems, cause different reactions to activities. What is right for me, may not be right for you, biologically, intellectually, emotionally, and aesthetically speaking.

Many people are unaware of the activity that can satisfy their own "biosocial" personality the most. I remember one woman who entered an upholstery class with great distaste at the entire idea. She couldn't afford to have her sofa done over so she decided to take it into the class and learn how to go through the process herself. She ended up with a reupholstered sofa and a new hobby because she had discovered an interest that was very enjoyable for herself.

Part of the search for self may be finding those interests that satisfy one's own particular nature. Once people discover the "sugar" that helps their own particular "medicine" go down, they should attempt to keep the interest going and not allow the pace and pressure of life around them to crowd it out. Everyone needs their own "island," or an activity that they can escape to, and return from refreshed. As a woman in one of my classes stated, "I don't allow myself to be drawn into just *any* activity. It must satisfy me in some way, and I don't want to be doing it to please friends."

First on the list of things to do in leisure should be the study of one's self. Time should be allotted for a self survey. This is not the painless way to spend one's spare moments, but it can lead to more contentment as one proceeds along with this self analysis process. "Know Thyself" is an old precept, but one quite important in the attainment of any real happiness in life.

In working with women through exercise and discussion, I have made several observations which may be worthy of mention. They are concerned with one's interests and how they affect personality.

First of all, it would appear that the woman with fewer interests is apt to be the woman most likely to be easily depressed or fatigued. On the other hand, where women have several interests, there seems to be a higher energy level and less of a tendency to become depressed.

Another observation is that there is a need of many women to seek identification for themselves. Betty Friedan has examined and explored this problem so well in *The Feminine Mystique* that I will not go into it any further here. I will add that this identification does not always have to be in a career. A woman can find identification in a multitude of non-vocational interests. She does have to be sure that they suit her own nature and personality if she is to truly find identification and fulfillment, however. She has to feel that what she is doing is not "silly" and is worthy of her energies. A vocation does not always insure fulfillment. Just because there is a salary and title does not mean that needs are being satisfied.

Another observation concerning the housewife involves self assertion. Maybe the role of housewife carries with it a large element of self denial, but it seems that this can be a little overdone. I have continually heard the statement that "My needs come last in our home, of course," or "What I want to do really isn't important. The children must have every opportunity to grow up into good adults." This type of comment is usually made cheerfully, but often wistfully.

Most housewives and mothers are not competitive in their activities with their family. Often the children know that mother is letting them win at monopoly or that she could play better badminton if she wanted to. Her husband may know that she can beat him at cards but doesn't. Everyone may be very happy about the entire proceedings, or they may feel that somehow there is not much spirit or enthusiasm in anything they do together.

To be the facilitator may be woman's role, but in following it completely she may be allowing a large part of her own life to go down the drain with the dishwater because her conscious or unconscious needs are not given expression. Perhaps the result of such maternal surrender comes about in the physically unexplainable headaches, the zestlessness with which she attends to her household chores, and the sudden tears that may come on without any obvious cause.

The housewife must submit to the demands of her household, but to what degree? Should there never be any self assertion? Must all of her hours, even those when she could arrange some leisure time for herself, be spent in thinking only of the needs of her family? Many women seem to be divided on this point. They feel that they should have interests, but also feel that to assert their personal interests is not to be adhering to the pattern of American motherhood. The result is that they appear to be waging some kind of war within themselves, striking out for freedom one moment and repressing any personal desires the next.

Women do have leisure time however, even though they may deny it. Some women spend this leisure in overextended coffee sessions. Other women spend their "leisure" in busy-work, puttering around the stove, or aimlessly gazing through magazines. Some housewifes lonesomely spend their spare time with a cup of coffee, others spend their free moments window shopping or dashing from one shop after another without buying anything. Then there is the woman who spends every minute free from housework or child care, in civic responsibilities. This is the woman who is so committed to committees that she couldn't find a moment to be lonely, or to become involved in coffee mornings.

Anne Morrow Lindbergh[3] feels that woman's life would be much richer if she could have a regular and enriching moment of solitude. She feels that many women do not know *how* to feed the spirit and so they try to muffle its demands in distractions. Woman's life is no longer one of simplicity, but one of multiplicity:

Distraction is, always has been, and probably always will be, inherent in woman's life.

For to be a woman is to have interests and duties, raying out in all directions from the central mother-core, like spokes from the hub of a wheel. The pattern of our lives is essentially circular.

In another chapter of her book, *Gift from the Sea,* Mrs. Lindbergh touches on recreation as a source of personality unification for the housewife:

Woman's life today is tending more and more toward the state William James describes so well in the German word, "Zerrissenheit—torn-to-pieces-hood." She cannot live perpetually in "Zerrissenheit." She will be shattered into a thousand pieces. On the contrary, she must consciously encourage those pursuits which oppose the centrifugal forces of today. Quiet time alone, contemplation, prayer, music, a centering line of thought or reading, of study or work. It can be physical or intellectual or artistic, any creative life proceeding from oneself . . . What matters is that one be for a time inwardly attentive.

One of the values of recreation is that it redirects attention from problems, and helps the individual to focus his attention on something else, either inside or outside of himself. Because recreation serves this function, and because it serves as a relief from regular routine, the housewife could use some carefully chosen, personalized recreation.

Distraction is one of the occupational hazards of being

a housewife. One writer in a recent *Time Magazine* article lists a few more. Valerie Goldstein,[4] speaking from a theological position states that the following are a few specifically feminine problems: Triviality; distractability; diffuseness; lack of an organizing center or focus; dependence on others for one's own self-definition; tolerance at the expense or standards of excellence; inability to respect the boundaries of privacy; sentimentality; gossipy sociability; mistrust or religion—in short, underdevelopment or negation of self.

That's a bit of a blow. Most of these qualities tend to proceed from the role of woman as a housewife and mother. In many cases the housewife may cling to this underdevelopment of self because she knows of nothing she could do other than housework.

I remember a class I conducted in which the above point was painfully made aware to me. I suggested that the future may bring "household helpers" to assist the housewife with her housekeeping functions and thus free her for more activities with her family and for self-development. These household helpers would be a core of workers, available for a minimal expense to the homeowner, who would come in several times a week for window washing, vacuuming, kitchen cleanup and silver polishing. I was expecting sighs of ecstasy and words such as "That would be too good to be true." Instead there was a long silence. The entire group looked stunned with the exception of a few women who looked upset. When I asked what they thought of the idea and if they thought they would want to pay 40 dollars a month for such a service, one woman replied shakily; "What would I *do* with all that free time?" The others began to panic in turn, each one stating that the world was becoming too effortless, that they felt that their job would be taken away by automation. One woman stated that the day would be a drag if she couldn't mop and scrub and sweep. Another said that then she'd feel obligated to spend more time with the children and they got on her nerves when she was with them too long. A woman who previously had always complained of fatigue now stated that she loved housework.

Many of the women who appeared to be quite stricken at the idea of their work being swept out from under their feet were women who had frequently been overheard complaining about all the work they had to do. They were women who declared "Our job is really useless. We do the same old thing over and over again. Clean the sink, a minute later there's something in it again. There's no goal reaching to housework." Other members of this particular group have often commented that much of their day was quite boring. One idea was suggested, to eliminate a large part of the more monotonous aspect of their work, and nobody was even slightly interested. They complained, but they wouldn't want it much different, afraid of the time that would require filling.

The question is: "What is there to do?" The answer is so large that it in itself can cause a panic. Choice is easier when there is less to choose from. In the present day and age, in almost every fair sized city, there is a multitude of activity opportunity. Choosing which is worthwhile depends on the needs and personality of the individual.

Activities exist for those interested in education, creativity, cultural enlargement, service, sports, outdoor life, social life, music, dance, acting or spiritual life. Great Books Institutes; Girl Scout leadership; theatre matinees; modern jazz dance classes; sculpturing; Sweet Adelines Women's Barbershop Quartettes; Audubon Society day trips to the mountains or streams; politics; collection of folk music, beer mugs or music conductors' autographs; American As-

sociation of University Women; Gray Ladies hospital days;
reading for pleasure—we could go on and on with the list
of possibilities.

Attitudes have to be changed a bit. Walking in the snow
with the four year old should be considered as worthy of
time expenditure as cleaning out the refrigerator. Lying
on the grass and looking up at the clouds with the eight
year old's Brownie troop has to be allowed to grow in one's
value system so that it surpasses the satisfaction achieved
from cleaning the picture window in the living room. What
about listening to a record of Robert Frost instead of watching three hours of morning television while the ironing
is done? Or how about making the physical fitness exercises
more interesting by inviting the next door neighbor in for
ten minutes of conditioners instead of one and one half
hours of coffee. (Incidentally, exercising can be fun if done
to music with a beat.)

Instead of spending the entire weekend working in the
yard, why not invest in a ping pong table or badminton set
and get to know the children better? Later, when the children are grown and have left, they may still come back to
visit their good friends—Mom and Dad. How many kids
never know what it is to have FUN with parents? Playing
together as a family may seem childish or a waste of time,
but not any more so than those long holidays when a
bored family is locked up together with nothing to do.

Many a housewife has creative urges which lead her toward painting the entire house and having everything
from the furniture to her nerves in an uproar, when she
could just as easily get a small sheet of canvas and do some
oil painting. Other women with an urge to get away will
jump into the car, drive ten miles to the big shopping area,
and return home with shattered nerves and angry feelings
about not being able to buy all those wonderful products

they saw. They could have spent a more enjoyable "get-away" afternoon riding a bicycle on a quiet road. Then there is the woman who bangs pots and pans around because she has a pent-up, trapped feeling. She could just as easily release her tensions by driving a golf ball 200 yards on a nice, sunny golf course, and socialize with a few friends at the same time. Of course for both bike riding and golf one needs a minimum of physical fitness if the activity is to be enjoyable. Women who raise children should get themselves into as fit a condition as possible anyway because child rearing itself can be a sport, and is not often played best by the weary.

We again return to the main thesis of this book—there is a great waste of what could be satisfying leisure time. In the housewife's case, a fear of leisure may be part of the reason that she wastes it. Our nation's Puritan past with its emphasis on work invades the twentieth century and will not let us relax or develop our abilities in leisure skills.

As a nation, we have evolved so well, that we have earned some extra hours. But we keep giving them back.

13.

The Golden Years

Life is long if life is full—SENECA

One of the most depressing areas of the leisure wasteland is that of the senior citizen. It is probably one of the most lonely and monotonous, though others mentioned in this book could compete quite strongly for those titles. One of the reasons that the lot of our older citizens is so depressing is the idea that retirement years should be the frosting on the cake of life. They are not. To many retired men and women their work was the frosting and their retirement, the crumbs.

It is common knowledge to undertakers that retirement is not the happy word that employers would like to have it be. As soon as the full impact of "leisure" is felt by the newly retired, he procedes to rapidly fade away. He has no reason to live, he wakes up one morning and realizes this, so he dies. Healthy, productive working men when viewed a year or so after retirement may not have the same glow of life and vitality that characterized them during the nine to five years.

In my first year of college I happened to live with my grandparents, who were going through the pangs of an empty retirement. They were both intelligent people, but for all that leisure time they could not come up with any intelligent ideas on what to do. At that time I wrote a short story called "The Unprepared" that seemed to portray their life as I saw it. Here it is:

The old lady sits alone by the window. She is crying inside, you can tell by her face. The atmosphere is filled with her loneliness. It has completely absorbed me and has stolen all enthusiasm for the studies before me.

The clock ticks on, announcing the creeping of time over years of nothingness. Five, ten, twenty years have been spent in the same nothingness. On ticks the clock. Where are the wonderful spiritual products of such leisure—the inspiration of a garden, the thrill of music, the warmth of friends, the happiness of handcrafts?

The old lady is breathing, but her life has gone. It had been a life of the wash tub, the scrubbing of floors, the raising of children. Her joys were those found in work. She had no time for foolish pleasures.

The studies in front of me are blurred by eyes filled with sympathetic misery. I want to help her. I want so much to show her the joys of life, the thrill of activity. I must do something! She is my Grandma! But we speak different languages. She would not understand mine.

"Live by the inch and not the mile," she had replied to my far flung imagination and ambitions. But that was years ago, when she was active and I worshipped her above all others.

"Oh, but Grandma, I want to do so much," I would cry.

"I want to play music, work in another country, play golf, act in Shakespeare, lead a Girl Scout troop . . . so many things I want to do."

I can still see her shaking her head as she'd say, "Poor Connie, we must be happy with what we have. It isn't necessary to go jumping over the fence in search of activity. It's pretty active on this side."

A chill sweeps through my back as I watch her at the window. "Oh, Grandma," my heart cries. "Are you still happy with what you have? Or do you wish you'd taken a look over the other side of the fence?"

Retirement is a dismal affair for many. The picture is getting brighter, however. Senior Citizen clubs throughout the country are really taking hold. From the sound of the laughter and song that comes from many of the clubhouses of these groups, it would seem that they are finding retirement to be the frosting that they had looked forward to for so many working years.

George B. Cutten is quite pessimistic about leisure and has written a book called *The Threat of Leisure*. In it he describes the two types of people preparing for leisure:

> Americans may be divided into two classes; there is one class (a growing class) which is composed of those who work moderately, take their vacation as they go along, and keep fit. . . . The other class works to the limit, needs a yearly vacation, and looks forward to early retirement to enjoy the closing years of life. It is doubtful how successful the latter class is.[1]

The fear of joining the ranks of the retired extends in many cases to those who have had a lifetime of hobbies and interests. Just recently a professor of recreation told me that she faced retirement with some trepidation. She was wondering about finding some sort of "purpose" to her leisure. Another person, a gentleman sitting near a Senior

Citizen clubhouse in Pasadena, told me he had taken up hiking and model making as a boy and had never given it up. When asked if he belonged to the group that was whooping it up in the clubhouse he sneared, "They'll never get me in that group. They never *do* anything. Oh sure, they sing and play shuffleboard, but what kind of a life is that for a grown person!" When asked if he didn't find the companionship an attraction he declared that he'd rather live apart than spend an entire day in "things that had no purpose."

It is this type of person that seems to suffer the most. The person who refuses to transfer his values from work life to leisure life, is the person for which leisure is a tedious bore. A change in attitude toward play is needed by all those dominated by the work ethic, but is especially needed by those retired whose entire day is free time. If they can only value themselves as human beings when they are on a payroll, or putting in 50 hours a week at some profession, their self image is going to be quite unattractive when they are among the unemployed. Leisure to them is not the pleasant word it could be.

Cutten also said:

The trouble is, we have been training men for tasks rather than for living. When these tasks are accomplished there is nothing for them to do, and they have no personal resources upon which to draw. Education is credited with the great success and the large results accruing from these accomplished tasks; must it not also be charged with the deficiencies in the personal development of the worker?[2]

But what about the physical and mental deterioration of the older person? How can they be very active when they have less energy, less interest, and are less physically fit? Dr. James E. Birren, chief of the section on aging of the National Institute of Mental Health, does not feel that there is *that* much loss of ability as a person ages. He has

made a survey of 47 healthy men aged 65 to 91 and found
that the keenness of an oldster grows considerably sharper
in the years between 72 and 77. He saw indications that
men in their 70's do not necessarily have a poorer memory,
poorer emotional responsiveness, or less ability to pay attention than men in their 20's or 30's.

It seems to be quite important in the mental health
process to fight the aging process—in other words, to not
give up. Dr. Birren found that many men in his study gave
themselves challenges just to demonstrate to themselves
that they still retained their physical and mental health.
These "denials of aging" or this rebellion against aging
"was found to be a useful reparative measure against
depression."

There is one area where the older citizen is quite vulnerable however. Dr. Birren's researches found that an older
man, as sharp and alert as his younger colleague will usually
be hit much harder in his mental outlook by shock such
as the death of someone he loves, or loss of his job. He
normally will not be able to snap back the way a young
man can. Then they tend to give up.[3]

It takes a golden boy then to enjoy the golden years.
It takes a fighter—one who will not accept the empty days
of retirement, but will go out and fill his time with social
life and solitude, activity and rest, learning and relaxing,
religion and dancing. The fighter will restore the balance
that retirement upsets. He will put into his new life all the
needed satisfactions of the old. He has needs for recognition, new experience, escape, companionship—and he
finds activity that will satisfy these needs.

Most of us have a rendezvous to keep with the Golden
Years. Some of us will make it an exciting affair. For
others—it will just be a no-return trip to the Leisure
Wasteland.

14.

The Bored Unmarried

Oh, to be young, happy, single and free as a bird
again! Then I was living!—THE CRY OF MANY
MARRIED WHO DON'T REMEMBER WELL.

There are many young, single working people who do
have the time of their lives. They spend each leisure hour
as fully as possible. They have friends, they laugh, they
learn, they move, they do. These are the people who say,
"Now I am on my own. I don't have the responsibilities
that I had living at home and I have not yet assumed the
responsibilities of marriage. I am going to use this time to
pack in as much as I can!"

Bertrand Russell said, "To be able to fill leisure intelligently is the last product of civilization." If the intelligent
use of leisure is associated with a stage of civilization, then
the young unmarried are in many cases living as the primi-
tives. They have all the tools for good living: Freedom,
youth, money not tied up in all manner of payments,
health . . . Why aren't they using this intelligently? Why

does there seem to be so much boredom, monotony and loneliness among the freshest of our human crop?

You may declare angrily that this is all nonsense. No one in their right mind would say that the young working person in our country today is discontent with his free time and has difficulty filling it. Just look around, and you shall see. Ask, and you shall find out. I've asked, and I've lived among them. As an owner of a girls' residence told me:

You wouldn't recognize these girls if you saw them on the weekend. They're well dressed and have attractive hair styles now because they are just getting home from work. But on the weekend they don't seem to care at all about what they look like and most of them drag around in an old robe and slippers all weekend long. They sleep until one o'clock both Saturday and Sunday mornings and then lay around on their beds for the remainder of the day. It's more like an old age home around here than anything else.

A cook in another girls' "club" told me:

I really have to laugh when I think about what the husbands of these girls are going to feel after their second week of marriage. How such attractive kids when fixed up can look so bad when off work is amazing to me. They just don't seem to be interested in anything—especially what they look like during their leisure hours around the house.

An Air Force officer told me that:

If the single fellows on base don't go out for the recreation program or go into San Francisco they just seem to sit around the barracks and mope. They don't know what to do with all those hours!

A Y.W.C.A. director states that:

The girls living here just don't seem to have enough conversational material. They talk about clothes and work and then they draw a blank.

Another girls' residence owner says:

Leisure activity! That's funny. These girls are just waiting to get married. Any time spent without boy friends is just a miserable period of time to be gotten through. Hobbies! That's a laugh!

A Y.M.C.A. director felt that:

These boys are just as lonely and shy as the girls. They don't seem to feel confident enough yet in a social situation and many of them sit around here much more than they go out on dates.

That's the unhappy side of the young, unmarried picture. This is the side that adds up to many leisure hours of isolation and loneliness. The lost weekend (lost in terms of boredom, not alcohol) seems to be a regular feature in the lives of many of our bored unmarrieds, as they go to their small, individual cells to recuperate from the week's work. In not a few cases the recuperation lasts longer than is necessary. What young and healthy body needs two complete days of sleep and lounging for every 40 hours of work? If that much rest is needed, a hospital would be a better place to go to than an unattended room.

Let's take a look at the weekend of our sweet, strong, young, free things. Friday night he/she is just too beat to "do" anything so there is a quick meal (often I have seen them fix themselves a bowl of cornflakes) and then down on the bed for a night of sweet sleep. The next morning the bored unmarried may wake up around noon feeling dull and sluggish. He may wobble as he goes to the bathroom to brush his teeth. This wobbly, sick, weak feeling may be interpreted as a need for more sleep, so after the face washing and coffee drinking ceremony is over, back to bed he will go.

Around dinner time he may get the urge to get up and get something to eat. After this meal he may feel like watching television instead of going out anywhere. This tires him out early and he dozes off on the sofa in the middle of a ten o'clock thriller. Sunday morning finds his system in a real state of weakness, so he can't make it to church. He spends the entire day with the newspapers, sprawled out on the sofa. By evening he's as cross as a frustrated grizzly bear and twice as ugly. (Take your own survey and see how many of the bored unmarrieds you will find in robe and slippers at three P.M., five P.M., or any other P.M. of the days of leisure.)

Lindeman, in his book *Leisure—A National Issue,* writes:

> Certainly, no reflective person desires that this vast amount of free time—22 percent of the total—shall become another manifestation of waste. Wherever there is waste there has been a prior lack of foresight and planning. But it is much more difficult to plan for leisure than for work because the usual pecuniary incentives are absent.[1]

Each individual should be free to choose his leisure in his own way, though there are many who have come to recognize the fact that there is great danger in free time without channels for expression. Just how free is the individual when it comes to leisure choice? When awareness of activities is limited, is there really very much freedom?

Many young unmarried have no idea of what there is to do. Many take the short cut and go to the nearest bar in search of exciting companionship. Often they find this not at all the fun that they thought it would be.

Then there are those who run from one activity to another, keeping quite busy and breathless. They are usually quite happy. Many are building up boredom insurance for the future and are learning such skills as art appreciation, love of literature, tennis, skiing, socializing, outdoor life, education for fun, creative activities like acting and painting. When the running and moving is just "fun for the moment" it is doubtful how much future enjoyment they are insuring. These may be just the people who do remember how much fun and freedom they had when young. Because of poor preparation, their future may never bring as much satisfaction as their "days of wine and roses."

Balance is very necessary for the activities of this young group of people, though they may not be aware at all of how important this is because they are having too much fun to think about anything. I recall a very snooty fellow who met this balance problem face to face in a two month period of his life. He had been attacked by some young hoodlums on the street and had suffered a broken leg. The leg took some time in healing, so he was forced to stay in bed for two months.

This fellow was an intellectual and always had a glorious time with his books. Every free minute was spent in art books, history books, literature and current events. When I visited him a week after the accident, I saw an extremely depressed individual. "You can't read all the time. It's just not possible for the brain. What a tremendous waste of time . . . to get tired when you *want* to read. My mind just stops absorbing and I get very tired, though I know I want to continue."

I suggested that he play some silly game, or watch a simple television program and he started his usual speech about the time that was wasted in activities that were not worthwhile. I told him that they may offer a change of pace and a better rest for the mind than just sitting and moping. He was willing to try anything, and after we had played a few hands of canasta he was ready to go back to Bacon, Thoreau, and Schiller. He began watching situation comedy shows and doing his arm and waist exercises. Balance was so restored that he began to feel that being bedridden was the only way to really live.

The young unmarrieds have a wonderful opportunity. The only excuse for their boredom is that they are not yet aware that there are things to do, and that it is up to themselves to get out of bed, and become involved in activities. They must balance the activities and they must experiment with many different interests instead of settling for the first one that comes along. This is their time. They may never be so free again.

Youth set loose should not enter the Leisure Wasteland. They have everything in their favor. But, many will enter the land of the leisure waster. Pity.

15.

The Harried Married

It takes a heap o' livin' in a house t' make it home.
—EDGAR A. GUEST[1]

Back at the ranch, things aren't going so well. Many a husband and many a wife is saying: "Oh, to be single again!" They recall the freedom, money and time they had to themselves. Now responsibilities and people are crowding in on them. Their leisure isn't their own.

They do have leisure, but it is "compromise time," in which they find a common denominator of activity which no one enjoys to any great degree and which is slimmed and trimmed enough to fit into an often starved budget. Usually the car payments, dentist bills and gardeners wage takes a bigger slice of the monthly pay check than recreation takes.

However, in spite of their divergent interests and limited resources, the family does spend two of its seven days *around* one another. Aware of the constant barrage of advertising declaring the fun and frolic of family leisure, oftentimes specific families cannot discover why they are missing out. And they have a vague feeling that they are.

Why aren't we living leisure like they do on our rose colored TV set, the family may ask. "Too much work around the house too be done. . . . too little money . . . the kids take too much supervision!" These are some of the excuses given for their leisure activity bankruptcy.

But the feeling of missing something lingers on. The garage may be filled with sports and camping equipment, books or craft materials, nature study materials and phonograph records. The car may be filled with gas—but past experiences of long hours spent on the freeway to the accompaniment of shrieking children's voices, quickly dispels the idea of any activity of that nature.

Decision on what to do together is often quite difficult. Everyone seems to want to do something different. So, rather than try to agree to something that no one really wants to do, the family in many cases chooses inactivity. They just waste or loaf through the day, a leisure pastime that has caused some children to comment "Sundays are so boring." Indeed they are in many homes where four or five people find themselves idly engaged in nothing. (If they love doing nothing that's something different. Much has been written in praise of idleness.)

Though "nothing doing" may rank high on leisure activities of the family, there are many other interests that are being carried on. In an Opinion Research Corporation study[2] of 5,021 persons it was found that "watching television"; "visiting with friends and relatives"; and "working around yard and in garden," were the leisure activities participated in most regularly.

In another study of 85 families,[3] the eight family activities which were most frequently engaged in were different from the nine activities reported from which "greatest pleasures were derived."

Most Frequent Leisure Activities	*Most Pleasurable Leisure*
1. Listening to radio	1. Movies
2. Visiting friends	2. Picnicking
3. Entertaining friends	3. Church
4. Attending movies	4. Fishing
5. Auto riding for pleasure	5. Visiting and entertaining friends
6. Eating dinners, breakfasts, suppers outside of home	6. Pleasure driving
7. Picnicking, barbecues	7. Watching television
8. Caring for home grounds	8. Sports
	9. Listening to the radio

The above study was done in 1952 when television was just getting under full sail, so perhaps listening to radio would be preempted today by tube watching. It is rather interesting to note that watching television or listening to the radio are way down (seventh and ninth place) on the list of "Most Pleasurable Leisure," while listening to the radio is top on the list of "Most Frequent Leisure Activities." It would appear that the respondents of this survey would rather go out than stay home, as most of the activities lead the respondent out of the house.

Another study, this one of 476 Catholic husbands and wives,[4] indicates that "outside activities" are given top priority in the category "best recreation between husbands and wives." The remaining eleven leisure preferences are now listed in order of their frequency:

Visiting or entertaining friends
Movies
Cards
Occasional night out alone
Sporting events
Dances
Dining out
Mutual home interests

Reading
Picnics and motor trips

It would appear that there is a strong interest in getting away from the ranch. You have to go way down on the list of above activities before you get to any home activities. This means that there are eight other interests that would be chosen before one would consider "Mutual home interests" as a possible leisure activity.

Why are we running from the home so fast? Hill, in a book called "Families Under Stress" has suggested one reason:

> The modern family lives in a greater state of tension precisely because it is the great burden carrier of the social order. In a society of rapid social change, problems outnumber solutions, and the resulting uncertainties are absorbed by the members of society, who are for the most part also members of families. Because the family is the bottleneck through which all troubles pass, no other association so reflects the strains and stresses of life. With few exceptions persons in work-a-day America return to rehearse their frustrations within the family, and hope to get the necessary understanding and resilience to return the morrow to the fray.[5]

Margaret Mead has suggested that because the center of existence has been shifted from work to the home, work will soon be considered only as a way to rest from the effort and stress of home life.[6] How many people today can hardly wait to get back on the job and rest up from the family?

What are all these causes of tension within the four walls of our ranch styled heavens that everyone would like to run from? There are many and they range all the way from money to personality differences.

Vance Packard[7] has suggested in *The Waste Makers* that our obsession for buying has tended to make us wasteful, debt-ridden and permanently discontented. There is always something to buy, we mustn't be satisfied with what we have . . . buy, buy, buy and keep America strong.

While we are keeping America strong, our family happiness may be getting weaker, however. Poor Dad may be overburdened with his part of the financial obligation. Mother may be constantly upset because she is making so many payments now that she can't buy that lovely new something or other she saw advertised in living color on her television.

The family is so wealthy in products and so lacking in dollars and sense, that there may be a bit of a guilty feeling if one doesn't stay home and gaze at the products and a rather sick feeling when one realizes they have no CASH with which to go anywhere or do anything. Once the family realizes that they are not much better off than indentured servants (bound to the credit company master) they may begin to detest all their lovely home products that, as Vance Packard has suggested, seem to wear out as soon as one has finished making the last payment. The family may then want to flee the scene, get away from the center of all their enslavement, not gaze upon the items that are keeping them (via payments) from bowling, skiing, going out to dinner and movies, riding horseback, or occasionally spending a weekend at some resort. They have no money to do these things, though they have plenty of good credit to keep them buying products. It is just this credit affluence that keeps them slaves.

One expert on marriage states, "The need to attain and maintain a plane of living that is out of keeping with the income is seen to be one of the major factors in creating major tensions for many families." Money can be a very painful problem.

Personality differences existing within a household can also be a very painful problem. Opposites may attract, but they can also frustrate. Take for example an afternoon of leisure time in which a family has decided to do something together and there are the following combinations of personalities interacting:

> The affectionate nature versus the unaffectionate
> The active person versus several sedentary types
> The doer (practical) and the thinker (idealist)
> Those who like to impress others and those who
> feel it's more honest to "be themselves"
> The culturally inclined versus the sports lover

There are many many other combinations of personalities that could come into active, open conflict if leisure were increased. As one woman told me:

> My husband and I are so different that we can't get along together if we are forced to be together for any long period of time. With more leisure time our life would be a constant battle ground. I am not asking for more leisure time.

Due to the circulation of people in our present society, people as different as may be imagined, can meet, and not having strong familial control, can decide to marry in spite of the tremendous difference in qualities they bring to the marriage. Koos says, "Any aspect of personality in which the couple is disparate serves as a focal point for tension or conflict." And it is in leisure that many of these tension games can be played.

Another study on leisure and family life would seem to indicate that satisfaction with leisure is closely related to general satisfaction in marriage.[8] Those who were not satisfied in marriage showed the following attitudes:

1. Dissatisfaction with the kinds of leisure.
2. Spending little of their leisure time with their partner.
3. Dissatisfaction because of financial restrictions.
4. Discord about matters of leisure activities.
5. Feelings that their marriage had deprived them of much fun because they had married before finishing school.

The results of this study, conducted among married students at Montana State University, tended to indicate that the *amount* of leisure time is relatively unimportant, but the *attitudes* concerning leisure time are significantly related to satisfaction in marriage.

According to physics, tension is a bonding agent. It may alienate hearts and minds, but it can keep people interested in staying together and battling for years and years. This warfare is naturally conducted in leisure time, when the family is together. I recall one house I entered on a marriage survey where I was verbally assaulted by one husband who declared, "Marriage ha! You can have it. I've been married for 35 years and I'm retiring from the struggle. So darn much talk about marriage and staying together. We've been married and miserable for 35 years!" He refused to participate in the survey of marital attitudes. It would have been interesting to have read his report.

Because of financial pressures and personality differences, many families have never spent a truly happy holiday or leisure period together. One woman vent her anger by telling me, "No, I don't like the holidays, because I do all the cooking all the time, they mess up the house all the time and we *never* seem to *do* anything together. And you should see the faces, down to here."

Let's look in on a little family gathering. It is the third day of a holiday period in the home of No-leisure-skill Johnson. Smoke from the fireplace and cigarettes has filled the room. The baby wants to be fed and is screaming and pulling at old Dad Johnson's balding head as he lies on the sofa. One soot blackened child is playing with a stick in the fire while another very bored looking teenager is slumped in an easy chair listening to his transistor radio. Mother is in the kitchen banging pots and pans around. The kitchen is filled with smoke too. Some gravy had caught on fire. The entire recreation program for this family has been to eat, and mother is a little upset that she has had to work continually so that they might have "fun" eating. (No one has had much fun eating as they are all feeling sluggish and bloated.)

One professor of marriage has come out quite strongly in favor of recreation as an aid to better family living.[9] He states that as marriages progress, responsibilities grow and recreation is sometimes neglected. This line of least resistance doesn't lead to the desired goal as recreation often provides the relish to married companionship that helps to keep it zestful. This authority feels that in some doubtful cases recreation may be just the touch needed to turn the balance in favor of happiness. This of course is taking into consideration whether or not the couple are already alienated from each other. If the emotional climate is at an unhealthy high it is doubtful whether a family recreation program is going to be of much assistance.

Lewis Terman found a positive correlation between the *happiness* score of both the husbands and wives (in his classic 1938 marriage study) and their degree of *participation* in outside interests together.[10] Burgess and Cottrell found the proportion of the "very happy" group in their 1939 study, who enjoyed all their outside activities together, to be "15 times as great" as those who engaged in few or none of their outside activities together.[11] This would be a very strong argument in favor of recreation as an aid in family mental health.

It may not be enough just to be together as a family. It's usually more fun (and tension relieving too) to take part in some kind of activity together. If the family is composed of a group of irritable, non-cooperating people, a game of cards, badminton or group singing to guitar may not help very much. But then again . . . maybe it will.

16.

The Talent Drop-outs

> Many people go throughout life committing partial suicide—destroying their talents, energies, creative qualities. Indeed, to learn how to be good to oneself is often more difficult than to learn how to be good to others.—JOSHUA LOTH LIEBMAN[1]

Next in our travels through the leisure wasteland, we come to a most pathethic sight. This is the talent drop-out. The talent drop-out is the fellow who *once* knew how to:

Play the piano
Read aloud well
Dance . . . social, ballet, square
Play basketball with the stars
Remember 30 lines of poetry, Shakespeare
Be able to appreciate the beauty of nature
Sculpt
Ski
Laugh
Respond to twist music
Look forward to eating
Ice skate, dive, bicycle, fence, sail
Sew, knit

Write short stories, poetry
Have a good time with people
Relax
Smell pine needles

Alas, but now all this has gone for the talent drop-out. Let us mourn together. A great part of a person has dropped by the wayside and now he stands bereft. The life that once breathed fire through the body has left. Talent has gone.

With so many people of talent, it seems almost a crime when a person deliberately walks away from some ability he has been gifted with or worked hard to develop. What are the excuses of this waster? Here are some most often heard:

I just don't have the time.
You have to grow up, throw away the toys.
The children take up so much time.
No money.
Involves too much practice.
I don't have any room for a piano.
My wife wants us to do everything together.
I *did* do that once, didn't I?
I'm getting too old.
Too many interruptions.
I work too hard to be able to relax enough.

There are all kinds of excuses, all of which add up to the demise of a talent. There must be moments in the lives of these talent drop-outs when they have a terrible pain right in the middle of their memories. They probably enjoy this nostalgia and wistfully long for the days when they danced for all the talent shows, or wrote prize winning articles for the school newspaper. Or perhaps they feel a real sadness when they recall the pride, joy in perfection, sense of aliveness and fulfillment that were part of their special abilities. "But there's no time now. I've got four hours of television to watch every night!"

In addition to the discontinuance of abilities, millions of others gradually discontinue the use of their senses of sight, sound, touch, movement, smell and taste. Consider the person who drives to work every morning without seeing anything beautiful around him. Or what about those who have forgotten what it is to smell the earth after rain, or leaves burning in the autumn. For many, the senses are dead and have been so for some time. This is a talent that has dropped away.

Helen Keller would have much to teach such a person about the appreciation of sight and sound. This blind and mute woman has found great beauty in her sense of touch:

I who am blind can give one hint to those who see: Use your eyes as if tomorrow you would be stricken blind. And the same method can be applied to the other senses. Hear the music of voices, the song of a bird, the mighty strains of an orchestra, as if you would be stricken deaf tomorrow. Touch each object as if tomorrow your tactile sense would fail. Smell the perfume of flowers, taste with relish each morsel, as if tomorrow you could never smell and taste again.[2]

Why should there be so many who cut off their abilities to see, hear, smell, taste, or enjoy movement? I recall a recent conversation with a group of people who were discussing their travels in Germany. One of the women was amazed when told that there were cobblestone streets, buildings with echoes, and musty smelling shops. "I can't remember any of that," she declared, almost as if accusing the rest of us of remembering things that weren't there. The thing that wasn't there seemed to be her senses. They were obviously out of commission.

Another obviously "sense-less" creature was recently observed as he was being taken by wife on a hike through the mountains. His head was down and he appeared to be thoroughly un-enjoying himself. This was something his wife wanted to do and he wasn't about to enjoy one minute of it.

A woman who lived in a sanitorium in Colorado for four years told me that all she could think about was getting out. When I stated that it must have been an awful place, she agreed, adding that it was supposed to have a beautiful view of the Rockies but she was so preoccupied with her illness that she hadn't time to enjoy scenery. Many a city dweller has deep longings to return to such a spot as that, but my shortsighted friend could only view the tragedy of her own "inner" world.

Many more examples could be found. The reader can probably find several areas of his own sensual world that are completely frozen and incapable of response because of lack of exercise. Such is the state of the senses of many who dwell in the Leisure Wasteland. Maybe now is the time to sharpen the senses and get out.

"But is there anyplace to go?" asks the gal who drinks her martinis dry. There are many places to go, and much to do. The opportunities for a very fulfilling leisure time are ample, and many people are not taking advantage of of these possibilities.

Wasted and unused areas of leisure actvity are *many*. Go up to the mountain trails to see the use they are *not* getting. Visit a Great Books Institute, ask how many people belong to this national organization and you will see how *many* people are missing out on this exciting "idea" exploration hobby. Explore the waste of tennis courts, archery ranges, concert programs, casting pools, riding trails, oil painting classes, library art film showings. Go to a local community theatre group production and see how many people are *not* taking part in this enjoyably demanding activity.

On the other hand, golf courses, boating marinas, night

clubs and public camping grounds are generally over-
crowded. Everybody seems to be cluttered up into a few
popular activities, leaving other "areas of leisure activity"
quite empty. It seems to be more of a question of "the
thing to do" than anything else, however. If casting pools
were suddenly declared the "in thing to do," there would
be a run on fishing equipment.

People want to know what there is to do, but they
seem to need approval from *Good Housekeeping* before
they will try it out. A few years ago an article on an old
Indian well appeared in a popular Western magazine.
Because of the publicity several thousand people headed
out into the desert to view this not very interesting bit of
remains. Nobody was overly delighted at what they found.

People need to worry more about their own needs
rather than what everyone else is doing. What is good for
one may not necessarily be good recreation for another.
People have to make an effort to find out what satisfies
their own particular nature. Effort on one's own does not
seem to be the "in thing" of today, however.

The psychiatrist Abraham Maslow[3] is very much concerned with the process of self-actualization, which is the
process of developing to a high level of perfection or fulfillment in certain activities. He has written a great deal
about "peak-experiences," or moments of great happiness
in which the individual feels intensely alive and functioning. These moments can come from being in love or while
listening to some particular music. Sometimes one has a
"peak-experience" while reading a book or seeing a painting or fully comprehending an idea. He feels "hit" by the
activity, very excited by it.

Maslow has asked people who have had such experiences
to describe the way they felt at such a time. Here are some
of the conclusions:

People in "peak" experiences

are more unified or "all-of-a-piece."

feel themselves to be at the peak of their powers, using all their powers to the fullest and best.

are more spontaneous, expressive, unrestrained.

experience a sense of effortlessness and ease of functioning.

are more free of past and future and most aware of living in the "now."

feel more poetic and rhapsodic in communication and expression.

This "peak" does not last long. Its intensity is enough, however, to be remembered and sought for again. This "peak" does not usually come when one is watching television, however. It usually comes when one is doing, or creating, or developing. Biographies and autobiographies abound with statements that sound like Maslow's "peaks."

We do not have to go to the great artists, writers or thinkers to find out about the joys that come from "creating." Ask a hobbiest who has just built his own car, written a short story, recorded his own reading of Poe, completed a sculpture or put together a model airplane. Talk to members of drama groups, chamber music quartettes, folk singing groups or poetry writing clubs. You will hear many raves of satisfaction because these people are engaged in activities that they love.

Some of the most excited people I have ever met are those who are "creating" a coin collection. They see their own work accumulating and being organized. They are developing an insight into the world's history and geography through coins. They are excited and the excitement is contagious. Talk to one and see. It would be difficult for even the most blasé of individuals to not feel the intense enthusiasm of the person who is "wildly" in love with his hobby, silly as it may appear to others.

For those who are developing talents, there are miles to go and acres to explore. The talent seekers and interest builders know this. They find that the more they develop themselves, the more energy seems to appear. In fact, most people with strong interests seem to have an inexhaustible supply of energy. Energy seems to produce energy.

Many people in the Leisure Wasteland ought not to be there. They are the people who have experienced an intense satisfaction, perhaps even a few "peaks," in some activity and then they proceed to forget all about it. One such person would be the fellow who goes golfing with a group of friends and finds that he really likes the sport. He vows to take it up wholeheartedly and buys a set of clubs, takes out a country club membership, and goes regularly with his friends to the golf course. One of his friends then moves to Seattle and another one gets transferred to another community and our new golf lover is left holding the clubs. These he promptly proceeds to pack away for once and for all and they never are seen again. The "big affair" is over, though ex-golfer may still be very fond of the sport.

Another example is the woman who visits a "Sweet Adelines" barbershop group for women. She sings her heart out and is rhapsodic about the singing evening for months afterwards—but she gets so busy that she fails to attend any other meetings. This was an activity that really "reached" her, but a few "busy work" duties caused her to give it up before she really got involved.

There is the person who gets an interest in model house making and is obviously in "heaven" as he sits with his glue and balsa wood. One day he runs out of balsa wood and forgets to ever go back to the hobby shop to pick up some more.

What is the matter with the people mentioned here? They enjoyed the hobby immensely. They felt, at the moments of performance, a rapture, a sense of wholeness they had not often felt before. Why did they give it up? Maybe it is just a question of values, and to play does not seem as important as other activities of our life. Perhaps we just have bad memories and fail to fully remember the joy of the experiences we like. It may be that we are afraid of "happiness." Life means serious business to some, and moments spent "pleasurably" may be considered wrong.

The future will bring much more leisure to spend escaping "pleasures" and talents. Many may consider hobbies and interests an extremely childish form of amusement. They may prefer to spend long periods of leisure in sleeping, or drinking in an adult fashion or in a kind of stylish boredom. In conforming to what they consider an adult attitude toward enthusiasm, interests and activities they may purposely extinguish their talents.

But let's move on. It is too sad. This acre of the Wasteland is filled with characters more hideous than those in Dante's *Divine Comedy*. They are the people who have subtracted substance from themselves. It is too horrible. Even Dante would shutter.

17.

The Waste of

Nervousness

One cannot be cured of stress, but can only learn
to enjoy it.—HANS SELYE, M.D.[1]

Intolerable stress leading to suicide will kill more than
19,000 in the United States this year.[2] Dr. Jack Ewalt,
psychiatrist at Harvard, gave these facts at a 1963 sym-
posium at the University of California Medical Center.
Selye says that some stress is good. That statement does not
suggest that a great deal of stress is excellent, and the Ewalt
figures would back that point up.

But why should we discuss such things as stress when
we are discussing leisure? For all who would like to keep
that word (leisure) holy, this constant attack upon its
virtues might be quite upsetting. Problems cannot be swept
under the carpet forever, however, and leisure time may
turn out to be "don't pass the buck" time. It will then be
that problems will force their way to the surface. Perhaps

this is one of the greatest values of work, the fact that it is a time in which one is occupied and can escape the stresses of their problems.

Repression is a very time consuming activity and is played often both in leisure and in work, though it is in leisure that it can really add up pain points. The feelings of nervousness, anxiety and stress all may be caused by messages from the subconscious saying, "I'm a problem. Face me." The unpleasant feelings result when repression answers "no," and pushes the problems back down, at the same time applying tremendous pressure to make sure that they won't come back again. It takes a great deal of energy to repress, and the result is that the repressed person is so preoccupied with this task that he has no time to do such things as relax, laugh, or develop a wholesome leisure activity.

Many people use the "spice" of recreation to keep from facing problems. Sports, crafts, reading, cultural or social activities should not be used as repressers either. These activities should be used to pick up or slow down tempo, to bring in solitude or to bring in people—in short, recreation should be used to balance and not as an escape from reality. Recreation has more important functions than to serve as a babysitter for problems.

So this brings the dilemma of problems right back to where it belongs—as a legitimate activity of leisure. Problem time should have as prominent a place in one's leisure schedule as the Garden Club or the Gun Association. When problems are given their *own time* they will no longer tend to sneak in and ruin all other activities. Problems are stubborn. They will persist until they are heard and they will intrude anywhere. By not recognizing them we cause a tremendous waste of leisure in our lives, because everything that we do is done in a preoccupied, or not wholehearted, fashion.

Problems create a great deal of nervous tension if not faced as they appear. Nervous tension can cause one to appear to be chased by demons. How many nervous people run from activity to activity, never settling on anything for more than a few moments, with their mind a thousand miles away. They have a feeling there's something to be done, but they don't know what it is. Drop a penny and they will act as though the noise has shattered every nerve in their body. Indeed the sound might, because every nerve is under a high state of tension and will continue to be so unless the problem is resolved or the body exhausted. Perhaps the person may be lucky to find an escape, allowing them to concentrate as fully as possible on something else for awhile.

Karl Menninger[3] has discussed nervousness in his book *The Vital Balance*:

We have said that under stressful conditions which may or may not be known to him or to others, an individual begins to "feel nervous" and to appear so to others. He feels tense, talks too much, laughs too easily, loses his temper frequently, seems restless and erratic in his movements, lies awake at night stewing over problems more or less real. . . .

Menninger says that this sort of nervousness can be identified by its relative mildness as there is not a great deal of interference with life activities and that the methods used to control it are merely exaggerations of those common to everyday life-coping methods. Here are some of the more common methods of coping with tensions as outlined by Menninger. Some are helpful, some only get the individual into further emotional trouble.

Hypersuppression (Conscious effort at self-control)
Hyperrepression (Inhibition)
Hypervigilance (Exaggerated perception)
Hyperemotionalism (Tearfulness, overgaiety, instability)
Hyperkinesis (Restlessness)
Hyperintellection (Worry)

Hypercompensation (Denial)
Somatic reactions (Minor somatic and sexual dysfunctions)

It all adds up to a great waste of leisure, as well as working time if the boss doesn't object too much. It is at highly nervous times that people are likely to take up such recreative measures as drinking, sex, dope, thrill seeking or escape through sleep. Sleep may turn out to be more of a wrestling match with tension than a relaxation.

Leisure, leisure . . . the golden time that man, down through the ages has dreamed of and worked for. Will it prove to be an empty dream? Instead of bringing happiness will it bring greater emotional pains than man has ever known before?

Will leisure bring more anxiety, or feeling that some misfortune is in store? Will we have more time to indulge in fears about taking responsibility . . . loss of possessions . . . old age . . . economic security . . . time passing us by?

There will be many possibilities for "anxiety knockouts." The following are some suggestions on how you may escape. Choose the one that best fits your own personality and will best aid you in getting away from vague feelings of uneasiness concerning yourself:

Wrong Approaches (My favorites)	*Check*
Gambling	_____
Sex without commitment, such as with pick-ups or prostitutes	_____
Aggression	_____
Hurting others through belittling	_____
Losing one's identity in large groups	_____
Isolation from people	_____
Ulcers, constant headaches	_____
Projecting one's own faults onto others	_____
Insomnia	_____
Thoughts of suicide	_____
Drinking all day long	_____
Egocentricity	_____
Bitterness	_____

Recent studies would seem to indicate that there is a little something wrong with each of us. The Midtown study, of 175,000 residents of midtown Manhattan found that only 18 percent of all the people interviewed showed no neurotic symptoms. 82 percent showed symptoms of disturbances ranging from mild to severe.[4]

According to a Chemical Engineering News survey,[5] one out of every twelve adults takes tranquilizers regularly. Add to this all the alcoholics, drug addicts and sex driven people, and you come to a rather startling number of real leisure wasters. Some of this is because of nervous tension, some of it is caused by other drives and needs.

There is a great deal of wasted time due to nervousness. Many people couldn't enjoy leisure even if they desperately wanted to. And the saddest part of it all is that they keep using the wrong escape techniques, thereby never escaping the tension wasteland. So they lift the glass high and give a toast, to the happy bygone days, and it seems to ease their tension.

18.

The Packing Away of Purpose

God, give me hills to climb,
And strength for climbing!
ARTHUR GUITERMAN

What ever happened to purpose? Instant indulgence seems to be the word today. Live in and for today. Be comfortable, satisfied. Be open to those around you and don't rise above the group. These are some of the slogans for living today.

Purpose seems to be a rather old fashioned word. People used to sublimate all their sexual and sensual drives into some kind of socially accepted purpose. This seems to be disappearing and the "pleasure now" principle is enjoying a fair degree of social acceptance.

Our pioneers needed purpose. All people building

countries need purpose. Have all our hills been climbed? If so, we can relax. But a people without purpose can become a deeply bored people, a "who cares" kind of people, a goal-less people.

Webster's Collegiate Dictionary defines purpose as:

1. That which one sets before himself as an object to be attained; intention.

Purpose gives a reason for living and a reason for living in turn supplies the energy for living. Perhaps this is why people who have interests and goals always seem to have more energy than those who have none. These purposes don't have to be consuming idealistic philosophies of life, but can exist in a practical, day to day form.

What are some examples of purposes that motivate man? What are some of these purposes that keep man working and striving? Here are a few:

Affiliation	— To be a friend, have friends.
Achievement	— To accomplish something, achieve a goal.
Sentience	— To enjoy the beauties of sight, sound, etc.
Fun Seeking	— To like to laugh, frolic, have a good time.
Understanding	— To want to find out reasons for actions or ideas, to explore and be curious.
Service	— To devote yourself to a cause. To help others.
Love	— To feel strongly about other people. To want and need them.
Health	— To enjoy feeling well. To be conscious of health foods, exercise.
Leadership	— To enjoy planning, organizing, guiding.
Creativity	— To produce, construct, make something.
Appearance	— To be concerned with the way one looks.
Spiritual	— To enjoy prayer, inspirational activities.

These purposes can overlap. One person can have more than one purpose. Too many people have none at all, however.

Many people today are experiencing the feeling of being

"driven" through life. They do not feel in control of their lives, but feel that they are definitely being led from day to day by forces beyond their control. They seem to be incapable of stating any strong purposes in their lives.

David Reisman[1] says we are heading away from being "inner directed" toward a state of being "other directed." Today's society may require a high degree of sensitivity from each individual toward each other. This doesn't mean that we can allow ourselves to run with the lemming. That tiny rodent runs hysterically into the sea, just because one started to run; the rest follow suit. "Other directed" behavior does not necessarily imply that one must be devoid of any "personal" purpose.

Life can be pretty dull without a purpose or two thrown in for spice. It can lead to a state of existence known as "joyless enjoyment." "Joyless enjoyers" make a career out of pretending. ("Pseudo" is another name for such people.) They engage in joyless enjoyment, hoping that no one will notice anything more than their raves about their "great love." Their primary satisfaction comes when they tell other people about their activities, although little or no joy is involved in the activity itself. There is a false joy in the impression that they make on others, however.

Joyless enjoyment is usually expensive. It involves costly sports equipment, heavy investment in crafts materials, several thousands of dollars output towards an all expense trip to Japan. It can cost a great deal in time as well as money. Things are paid for and not enjoyed, great effort is expended with no satisfaction return. But this is part of the joyless enjoyment game. How did this ridiculous situation come about?

Maybe advertising is responsible for the current popularity of joyless enjoyment. The average person watching his television or driving down the highways, is overwhelmed with a barrage of brightly colored advertising urging him to buy. Worse than the financial burden that such constant purchasing may impose, is the sense of guilt that he surely feels when he realizes that he will never be able to find time to use all that equipment. He then proceeds to hide some of this loot, hoping that by not seeing it, he will forget his inability to use it. He may stash it in the attic, basement or garage, but he cannot help bumping into it occasionally and remembering. Maybe because he is keeping up with the Jiltons absolves some of the guilt, or perhaps he feels that because he has the equipment he too is an artist or an athlete. We buy, but there is no purpose other than consumption. In many cases we *never* use the products purchased.

Clifton Fadiman[2] has a comment to make on this problem of possessing too many products with too little enjoyment of them. He says:

> We are suffering from an excess of stimuli, available everywhere and at all times. The lackluster faces of the subway rider reading his newspaper, the vacant look of the moviegoer emerging from his dark cave . . . these are all pictures of a special boredom. Not unhappiness, not fatigue, and certainly not aristocratic ennui; but that odd modern *stunned* look that comes from a surplus of toys and a deficiency of thought.

Clifton Fadiman has a suggestion for the improvement of this problem. He says that we must try to learn "play" of the mind. This mind play is a necessary activity we should learn to cultivate if we want to eliminate tedium as part of our lives. We have the products of a wealthly nation, now we must learn to play with them. And another important point . . . we must let our mind, heart, and soul become involved in our "play." If we don't, there will appear the joyless enjoyment that comes when only the physical body takes part in an activity.

There are many examples of people who are regular

joyless enjoyers. For instance there is the case of a 55 year old man with whom I recently spoke. He told me that his only leisure activity was television, but that he did not consider it an enjoyable activity. This was a non-drinking, non-smoking, non-napping individual who stated that he was not fond of being with people because he wasn't much of a talker. When I suggested that he sell the television and learn how to enjoy life rather than merely sitting through it he said, "Are you kidding? What would I do with all that free time? I'm not a television enthusiast, but it helps pass the time."

Another example is that of a family of five who take regular Sunday afternoon outings to the mountains or desert. The oldest daughter always gets sick, the son becomes irritable and cranky, father is always upset with the traffic and mother is so tired by the time she gets home that she doesn't want to prepare dinner. They all feel that they *should* get away and do something together on Sunday, but nobody enjoys or even likes what they do.

There is the case of the young married couple who feel it necessary to get out and visit people one day a week. They usually go to the home of another young married couple, where they watch television together. The husband states that when they arrive the television is on and sometimes their friends don't even come to the door but just mumble "Hi" from the sofa. He states that he feels they don't exchange more than 10 sentences all evening. "What else is there to do?" he adds.

Not knowing what else to do is a frequent reason for joyless enjoyment. The activity is a mere prop, set up to keep people from facing the fact that they can think of nothing to do. They can become quite frightened when this prop is taken away, without being able to quickly substitute another one.

There is a ready-made purpose allied with one's vocational life. It is to get the job done, to receive an income, to spend a certain number of hours in a place of business. Leisure has no such built-in purposes. Then it is up to the individual to give it a purpose, or to spend it without purpose. Great amounts of leisure given to masses of purposeless individuals can be a frightening thought.

It's time to unpack purpose and get it into operation again. Leisure time should be filled with a sense of purpose if we are to have any sense of *living* at all. There are substitutes for purpose that come in bottles, television tubes, and wild living . . . but let's not go into all that again. Just look at your own leisure, and see if it has any meaning at all to you.

19.

The Culture Clunks

They do me wrong who say I come no more
When once I knock and fail to find you in,
For every day I stand outside your door
And bid you wake, and rise to fight and win.
WALTER MALONE[1]

The culture-less clunks have mastered the art of letting opportunity fly by. In our society today we are surrounded by opportunity. Free concerts, art galleries, libraries, museums, adult education centers. Free cultural opportunities for all. Come and get it.

Culture wasters allow opportunity to knock its knuckles to the bone. They are usually not aware of wasting anything at all. You can't miss what you've never known, the saying goes.

Let's take a fictional look at some of these clunks, and see what their attitudes toward opportunity are.

Lines A Clunk Would Say

Merry Clunk: "We used to laugh in school when Mrs. Fox read Shakespeare. She'd get so carried away that none of us really listened to the words or got the meaning. I still laugh whenever I hear any Shakespeare today."

Sleepy Clunk: "The museums are lovely, damp and deep. But they make me sleepy."

Mad Clunk: "Don't tell me I'm missing out on the better things of life. I work hard. A six pack and TV are fine for me."

Prude Clunk: "I went to what was called an "art film" and was I shocked. Don't you tell me of the cultural values involved. It was nothing but a dirty old movie."

Ima Clunk: "Modern poetry is an insult to an intelligent creature. After all these years of the development of the symbolic tool, and this e.e. cummings rebel has to cast away all punctuation and capitalization. Who does he think he is? And what on earth is he trying to say?"

Will Clunk: "The libraries are NOT free. Everytime I go I have to pay a fine!"

Yura Clunk: "I've always wanted to associate with thinkers, like Plato did in his Platonic relationships, so I joined a Great Books group and found that thinking can be more sport than relaxation. I like my intellectual time to be more peaceful!"

Nica Clunk: "I'd go to more concerts in the park, but there are so many drunks on the benches."

Joan Clunk: "Coming from Great Falls, Montana, I wanted to become more worldly when I moved to St. Louis. So I joined a German class in which I was immediately made to feel like an isolate because of the way I pronounced things. I'm through with anything cultural from now on."

Bored Clunk: "Going to concerts is just snob appeal. Who ever heard of anyone actually liking three hours of that stuff?"

Laufa Clunk: "I'd go to operas more but I always get the giggles in the quiet spots."

20.

"Why, Why, Why"
—A Check List for
Waster Excuses

Why do we fail to make use of what we have? In many cases our excuses are just the easy way out. People without much time, money, friends or health can use these lacks to explain why they waste their leisure time. This is just an excuse, for people who have all the ingredients of the "good life" are also among the ranks of the leisure wasters.

What is the real reason for wasting the time that is ours, that is (or could be) free time, for our own direction and use. Perhaps it has to do with how each of us value ourselves. Obviously it is connected with how we value our leisure.

Consider the people who like to get up early on the week end because they have interesting things to do. Other people sleep late, stating that they need the rest. It is probably because they have nothing interesting to do. This person postpones all the household clean-up chores until the week end. This shows you how such a person values leisure. It is not special, but a place to dump all the unpleasant tasks of life.

What are these excuses? Investigate those most frequently used and see if they are not just ways you protect yourself from the unpleasant fact that you are allowing a large part of your leisure life go down the drain.

Check List for Leisure Waster Excuses   *Check*

I don't have enough time (and the little I have I want to
    waste as I please) .... _____

I don't know what there is to do .... _____

My mate would be upset if I wanted to do things on my own
    part of the time .... _____

I don't know anybody to do anything with .... _____

I don't have any money for recreation .... _____

I feel that it is wrong to think of enjoying this world. To seek
    happiness is evil .... _____

Life means to work. Play is a bit childish .... _____

I just want to be alone, and out of it .... _____

I don't know what I need to be happy .... _____

I don't have any energy or enthusiasm. I wasn't born with it.
    I'm the bored type .... _____

I never seem to plan ahead and when leisure comes it's too _____
    late to really arrange ....

No one I know has the same interests I have .... _____

I have no leisure. There's too much work .... _____

I can't get along with my mate. I don't want more time to
    fight and argue .... _____

I'm in a rut and can't get out .... _____

I'm sure I wouldn't be any good at balancing my activities
    and as a result I get bored stiff staying with one thing.. _____

I'd rather work and make money .... _____

21.
Ways Out of the Wasteland

There is a pathway out of the Leisure Wasteland (if anyone really wants to go). There are routes that lead to mental and physical exhilaration. One has to follow the signs however, for many routes only lead into other areas of the Wasteland.

Also, the way is quite difficult, especially for those who have developed weak thought and body muscles because of too much "living" on the living room sofa. Our easy living is not conducive to the effort that it may take to get ourselves out of a rut and into the road to "life" again.

Our twentieth century offers us everything in the way of comfort and ease. . . . Remote controls for the television and garage . . . intercoms in our homes . . . family room for mess-up and living room for dress-up . . . auto air conditioning . . . traveling bar-cases. If you can think of it you can buy it; comfort for sale at 20 different payments a month.

How do you escape the dubious happiness that our modern standard of living has brought us? How can we escape the knowledge that inside, many of us are as bare of interests and joy of living as an inmate in an isolated prison. It is easy to escape the inner barrenness when our environment is so cushioned and tranquilized through all the good things money can buy.

Are we really so terribly happy? Our popular songs would seem to indicate that we have a great need to dwell on sadness. I remember entering a restaurant and hearing a very sad song sung by one of the most popular singers of our day. In the restaurant were an assortment of people, including a woman in her 70's, a ten-year-old girl, and a male executive type with his wife and three children. These people were reacting to the music most interestingly. They seemed to cling to the juke box, at least all their attention was turned toward it. They all looked as if they were responding very strongly to this shrieked tale of woe. What the three children; ten-year-old girl; and 78-year-old woman were experiencing is a subject for the psychologists. Obviously they were thoroughly enjoying their misery, proven, I thought, when the song ended. The middle-aged executive stated, "That's a hell of a good song," and with the strong approval of the restaurant's band of musical mourners, started the musical sadness all over again, when he put another dime in the machine

I left the restaurant with the feeling that life indeed was tragic, and that love dropped out of one's life like bananas in a windstorm. Maybe the reason that so many find themselves in the Leisure Wasteland so often is because they enjoy their misery as much as they enjoy any happiness that may come their way.

But how do we get out of here? Where's the road away from misery? How can we get away from a perpetual wasting of all our free time? From one who's taken the trip (several times), here are a few suggestions:

This Way Out ⟶

1. Set aside *definite times* for leisure activity. (Don't let recreation come when it will. There are too many missed connections as a result of this kind of non-planning.)

2. Make *use of recreational products* instead of mere purchase with later neglect.

3. *Eliminate things that bore* you in leisure time.

4. Carve out a place in your *budget for leisure* activity. (Don't spend the weekend doing nothing, because you feel obliged to gaze at the washer, dryer, rugs and sprinkler system, products which are taking up most of the paycheck in monthly payments.)

5. *Explore.* (Be a leisure pioneer and see what's out there in the leisure fields.)

6. *Experiment.* (Try out different types of leisure activity.)

7. *Educate* yourself for leisure skills. (Go to public classes, clubs, private lessons.)

8. *Transfer some values* of work to values of play. (Make friends through leisure activity as well as work. Get a feeling of belonging through a leisure interest as well as through work. Transfer some achievement values of work to leisure.)

9. *Destroy as many conflicts* and pressures as possible. (These tend to fragmentize one's life and fatigue one so that he or she is unable to enjoy leisure fully.)

10. *Stop making excuses* for not using leisure. (Face the fact that you do, or could, have some leisure time.)

11. Make a list of *free fun*. (You may be surprised to find out that it can become longer than expensive recreation.)

12. *Be with people.* (Don't let city living isolate you.)

13. *Break with people* who bore, who use, who belittle, who inhibit the expression of your real personality. (Put people in your life who add something to it.)

14. *Don't be afraid of baby sitters.* (If you have children spend some of your income on a baby sitter as well as for household appliances. You and your spouse may be happier with one night out a week than with the $40 monthly payment for wall-to-wall carpeting.)

15. *Spend some time to think.* (Think about who you are, what you want and if you're going at it in the right way. Leisure can be a great time for reflection such as this.)

16. *Learn to appreciate* literature or music or art or dance. (Develop some kind of interest that will give you mental or emotional revitalization.)

17. Remember this *leisure health triad*:

Health (Physical activities, rest
and proper nutrition)

Social   Solitude

(Include some health, social and solitude activities in your leisure time. The amount depends on your own personality, but most people need to consider activities for health, having time alone, and being with people—if they are to have a well rounded existence.)

18. *Question, seek, struggle and feel stress.* (Don't escape from these things in your leisure time, but face them.)

19. Remember that *recreation is an attitude.*

20. Remember that *recreation is an easy thing to let*

slip. (And often this is the ointment that helps smooth some of the tensions of life.)

21. *Participate.* (Don't take the easy, pasty-faced, jelly-muscled existence that comes from too much sitting on one's adipose tissues.)

22. *Heal.* (Diagnose your needs and prescribe a recreational treatment when tired minds, bodies and spirits need treatment. This may take a little experimentation.)

Notes

Chapter 1

1. Max Kaplan, *Leisure in America* (New York: John Wiley & Sons, Inc., 1960), p. 4.
2. The Royal Bank of Canada Monthly Letter, "A Business Man's Leisure," Quoted by Charles K. Brightbill, *Recreation* (New York: Prentice-Hall, Inc., 1953), p. 75.
3. Quoted in *Mass Leisure*, Eric Larrabee and Rolf Meyersohn (Glencoe, Ill.: The Free Press, 1958), p. 357.
4. Walter Gerson, "Leisure and Marital Satisfaction of College Married Couples," *Married Family Living*, November 1960, pp. 360–361.
5. Robert MacIver, "The Great Emptiness" in his *The Pursuit of Happiness* (New York: Simon and Schuster, Inc., 1955).
6. S. De Grazia, "Tomorrow's Good Life," *Teacher's College Record*, April 1960.
7. Jay B. Nash, *Spectatoritus* (New York: Sears Publishing Co., 1932)
8. Russell Lynes, "Time on Our Hands," *Harper's Magazine*, July 1958, pp. 34–39.

Chapter 2

1. Norman Lobsenz, "Pleasure Neurotics," *Science Digest*, August 1962, pp. 36–42.
2. *Ibid.*

3. *Ibid.*
4. From article by Harvey Swados, "Less Work—Less Leisure," *Nation,* February 22, 1958, pp. 153–58.
5. David Riesman, *Individualism Reconsidered* (New York: Doubleday & Company, Inc., 1954), pp. 126–27.
6. William Faulkner, cf. *Paris Review,* as quoted in *Mass Leisure, op. cit.*
7. Bertrand Russell, *In Praise of Idleness and Other Essays* (George Allen & Unwin, Ltd., 1935)

Chapter 3

1. Lynes, *op. cit.*
2. W. Heron, "Pathology of Boredom," *Scientific American,* January 1957, p. 52.
3. Aldous Huxley, *On the Margin; Notes and Essays* (New York: Harper & Brothers, 1923)
4. "Uncontrolled Boredom Can Sicken the Body," *Pasadena Independent Star News,* August 4, 1964.
5. *Ibid.*
6. From section on Fromm, *Theories of Personality,* Calvin S. Hall and Gardner Lindzey (New York: John Wiley & Sons, Inc., 1957), pp. 128–29.
7. B. De Voto, "Heavy, Heavy What Hangs Over?," *Holiday,* March 1956, pp. 36–9.
8. Clifton Fadiman, "Boredom, Brainstorms, and Bombs," *Saturday Review,* August 31, 1957, pp. 7–9.
9. "Uncontrolled Boredom Can Sicken the Body," *op. cit.*

Chapter 4

1. Charlotte Buhler, quoted in *Leisure and Aging* by Robert W. Kleemeier (New York: Oxford University Press, 1961) pp. 378–9.
2. "How to Lose Friends by Really Trying," *Time,* May 31, 1963, pp. 35–6.
3. Clifton Fadiman, *op. cit.*

Chapter 5

1. Harvey Swados, *op. cit.*
2. David Riesman, "Leisure and Work in Post-Industrial Society," found in *Mass Leisure, op. cit.*
3. Nancy C. Morse and Robert S. Weiss, "The Function and Meaning of Work and the Job," *American Sociological Review,* 20, 1955, pp. 191–98.
4. Bertrand Russell, *op. cit.*
5. Florence Greenhow Robbins, *Sociology of Play, Recreation, and Leisure Time* (Iowa: Wm. C. Brown Co., 1955)

6. Robert M. MacIver, *The Pursuit of Happiness* (New York: Simon and Schuster, Inc., 1955).
7. Arthur Newton Pack, *The Challenge of Leisure* (New York: Macmillan Co., 1934).
8. Charles K. Brightbill and Harold D. Meyer, *Recreation* (New York: Prentice-Hall, Inc., 1953), p. 37.
9. George B. Cutten, *The Threat of Leisure* (Columbus: American Education Press, 1933)
10. William C. Menninger, "Recreation and Mental Health," *Recreation Magazine*, November 1948.
11. James A. Wylie, "Education for Leisure," *Journal of Education*, October 1960.
12. Martin Neumeyer, *Leisure and Recreation* (New York: Ronald Press, 1958)

Chapter 6

1. Erich Fromm, *The Art of Loving* (New York: Bantam Books, 1956), pp. 1–2.
2. *Ibid.*, pp. 20–21.
3. Kahlil Gibran, *The Prophet* (New York: Alfred A. Knopf, 1955), p. 64.
4. William C. Menninger, *op. cit.*
5. Marian Chace, Director of Music and Dance at St. Elizabeth's Hospital in Washington D.C. "Psychological Aspects," presented at convention.
6. Helen Hall Jennings, *Leadership and Isolation*
7. Margaretha A. Ribble, *The Rights of Infants* (New York: Columbia University Press, 1943)
8. Smiley Blanton, M.D., *Love or Perish* (New York: Simon and Schuster, 1956), preface.
9. *Ibid.*, p. 7.

Chapter 7

1. *Business Week*, January 1963
2. U.S. Department of Commerce figures, printed in "Education, Recreation, and Consumer Forecast," *Overview*, December 1960.
3. *Time Magazine* article, April 24, 1964, p. 74.
4. "Family Life Weakens," *Christian Century*, June 26, 1963, p. 821.
5. Benjamin Seebohm Rowntree and G. R. Lovers, *English Life and Leisure* (New York: Longmans, Green & Co., 1951)
6. "Love's Long Leap," *Time Magazine*, December 13, 1963, p. 44.

Chapter 8

1. Louis P. Thorpe, Barney Katz and Robert T. Lewis, *The Psychology of Abnormal Behavior* (New York: The Ronald Press Company, 1948), pp. 18–19.

2. G. H. Mead, *Mind, Self and Society* (Chicago: University of Chicago Press, 1934)

3. H. S. Sullivan, *Interpersonal Theory of Psychiatry* (New York: Norton, 1953)

4. E. H. Erikson, *Childhood and Society* (New York: Norton, 1950)

5. C. G. Jung, *The Undiscovered Self* (New York: Mentor, 1957)

6. Paul Tillich, *The Courage to Be* (New Haven: Yale University Press, 1952)

7. Henry A. Murray, *Explorations in Personality* (New York: Science Editions, Inc., 1962)

8. G. Murphy, Personality: *A Biosocial Approach to Origins and Structure* (New York: Harper, 1947)

Chapter 9

1. Florence L. Meredith, *The Science of Health* (Philadelphia: The Blakiston Company, 1942), p. 185.

2. Edward Bignell, quoted in *Independent Star News* (Pasadena), "Thousands are Playing it Cool," January 1, 1964.

3. Paul Dudley White, *Time Magazine*, November 29, 1963, pp. 52–53.

4. Gene Tunney, "It's More Fun to be Fit," *Reader's Digest*, February, 1942.

Chapter 10

1. E. J. Kepler, M.D., "Chronic Fatigue," Proc. Staff Meeting, Mayo Clinic, 17:340–344, 1942.

2. R. W. Husband, *General Psychology* (New York: Farrar & Rinehart, Inc., 1940)

3. F. L. Goodenough, *Developmental Psychology* (New York: D. Appleton-Century Company, Inc., 1934)

4. R. Dodge, "The Laws of Relative Fatigue," *Psychological Review*, 24:89–113, 1917.

5. R. B. Cattell, *General Psychology* (Cambridge: Sci-Art Publishers, 1941)

6. L. H. Lanier, "An Experimental Study of Affective Conflict," *Journal of Psychology*, 11:199–217, 1941.

7. F. N. Allan, "The Differential Diagnosis of Weakness and Fatigue," *N. England J. Med.*, 231:414–418, 1944.

Chapter 11

1. Will Durant, *Story of Philosophy* (New York: Pocket Books, Inc., 1954)

2. *Ibid.*

3. *Selected Essays of Francis Bacon* (New York: Appleton-Century-Crofts, Inc., 1948), p. 67.

4. Cited by Martin Neumeyer, *op. cit.*, p. 196.
5. Eduard C. Lindeman, *Leisure—A National Issue* (New York: Association Press, 1939)
6. Jay B. Nash, *Spectatoritus, op. cit.*
7. G. Ott Romney, "Recreation—It's Paramount Importance," quoted in *Recreation, op. cit.*
8. E. V. Pullias, "A Psychologist Looks at Recreation," *Journal of Health, Physical Education and Recreation*, November 1957.
9. S. R. Slavson, *Recreation and the Total Personality* (New York: Association Press, 1946)
10. Carl Jung, *op. cit.*

Chapter 12

1. John Howard Payne, "Home, Sweet Home."
2. Betty Friedan, *The Feminine Mystique* (New York: Dell Publishing Co., Inc., 1963)
3. Anne Morrow Lindbergh, *Gift from the Sea* (New York: Signet Book, 1955)
4. Valerie Goldstein, "Male and Female Theology," *Time Magazine*, June 27, 1960.

Chapter 13

1. George B. Cutten, *op. cit.*
2. *Ibid.*
3. From the *Sacramento Bee*, "If You are Growing Old—Fight—Do Not take it Lying Down," November 29, 1963.

Chapter 14

1. Eduard Lindeman, *op. cit.*

Chapter 15

1. Edgar A. Guest, "Home."
2. A survey for motion picture association of America, Inc., "The Public Appraises Movies," done by Opinion Research Corporation, December 1957.
3. Harold Hawkins and James Walters, "Family Recreation Activities," *Journal of Home Economics*, October 1952.
4. Hugh Dunn, "A Study of Some Catholic Marital Attitudes" quoted by Alphonse H. Clemens, *Marriage and the Family* (New York: Prentice-Hall, 1957)
5. Reuben Hill, *Families under Stress* (New York: Harper and Brothers, 1949)

6. Margaret Mead, "The Pattern of Leisure in Contemporary American Culture," *The Annals of the American Academy of Political and Social Science,* Vol. 313, September 1957.

7. Vance Packard, *The Waste Makers* (New York: Pocket Books, Inc., 1963)

8. Walter Gerson, *op. cit.*

9. Ray E. Baber, *Marriage and the Family* (New York: McGraw-Hill, 1953)

10. Lewis M. Termin, *Psychological Factors in Marital Happiness* (New York: McGraw-Hill, 1938), p. 181.

11. Ernest W. Burgess and Leonard S. Cottrell, *Predictions of Success or Failure in Marriage* (New York: Prentice-Hall, 1939), p. 62.

Chapter 16

1. Joshua Loth Liebman, *Peace of Mind*

2. Helen Keller, "Three Days to See," *Atlantic Monthly,* January 1933.

3. Abraham Maslow, *Toward a Psychology of Being* (Princeton: D. Van Nostrand Company, Inc., 1962)

Chapter 17

1. "How to Handle Stress: 'Learn to Enjoy it,'" *Time Magazine,* November 29, 1963, p. 52.

2. *Ibid.*

3. Karl Menninger, *The Vital Balance,* 1963.

4. "Are You Tense, Here's Why," *Science Digest,* June 1963, pp. 85–90.

5. *Ibid.*

Chapter 18

1. David Reisman, *The Lonely Crowd* (New York: Doubleday and Company, Inc.)

2. Clifton Fadiman, *op. cit.*

Chapter 19

1. Walter Malone, "Opportunity."